EATING BETTER FOR LESS

On the way home from a lecture on "Natural Foods and the World's Shrinking Resources," Yvonne Baker rebelled. She was tired of hearing alarming statistics. She wanted some answers. Weren't there practical, fun ways to conquer these dilemmas in an ordinary kitchen? She vowed to find a way that she, as an individual housewife, could improve her family's eating habits and at the same time consume less of the world's food supply.

In this book Yvonne Baker explains how you can become a better steward of God's resources—and also plan meals for your family that are appetizing, nutritious, and inexpensive.

YVONNE G. BAKER is a recognized authority on natural foods. She owns and operates the Colorado Springs School of Natural Cooking and is a foods columnist for the *Colorado Springs Sun*.

A winner of the General Foods national contest for writers of nutrition in 1977, Yvonne often caters natural foods meals. Her speaking appearances and natural foods classes extend beyond Colorado to include other parts of the country.

FROM GOD'S NATURAL STOREHOUSE

Practical alternatives to cooking with junk

Yvonne G. Baker

David C. Cook Publishing Co.

ELGIN, ILLINOIS—WESTON, ONTARIO
FULLERTON, CALIFORNIA

ACKNOWLEDGMENTS

In reality, the writer of a book plays only one part in its composition.

Special thanks go to the following people for their contributions to the formation of the book:

—To Denny Rydberg, who began the whole process of turning ideas into a book by saying, "I think what you're telling me would make an excellent book."

—To the *Colorado Springs Sun* and a wonderful editor there, Catherine McCormick, for years of help and encouragement and for first publishing many of the recipes and ideas that appear in this book.

—To Richard, my husband, who cheerfully tried all the recipes the first time and did the dishes afterwards.

—To the very kind and helpful people at David C. Cook who made working on my first book a delight.

—Most of all to my cooking class students for their constant pleas that I write a cookbook, for their hints and encouragements, and especially to the people listed below who tested and commented on all the recipes included:

Barbara Solanki	Gladys F. Savage
Rhonda Savage	Debbie Robinson
Kathy McCann	Casey Kohler
Ele Bromund	Marie Downing
Cynthia J. Groom	Carol A. Ransom
Maria Faulconer	Anne Threlkeld
Linda Kuster	Susie K. Harburg
Joyce Lyn Watson	Kathy Ferris
Hannelore Jend	Helen Jane Mummery
Delores S. Schoenherr	

FROM GOD'S NATURAL STOREHOUSE
© 1980 David C. Cook Publishing Co.

All Scripture quotations are from the New American Standard version unless otherwise noted.

First printing Jan. 1980
Second printing Feb. 1980
Third printing Apr. 1980

Published by David C. Cook Publishing Co., Elgin, IL 60120
Cover and inside design by Wayne Hanna
Cover photo by Jim Whitmer
Printed in the United States of America
ISBN 0-89191-818-3
LC 79-53976

To Richard, my husband

Contents

Part One
Eating Naturally

1
Why I Changed My Way of Cooking

The speaker began quoting statistics. Did we know that it took seven pounds of grain to make one pound of meat? Did we realize that our dogs ate better than many of the world's humans? Were we aware of the resources that went into those fast-food hamburgers?

The hamburger I'd eaten hurriedly to get to the lecture on time was feeling heavy in my stomach. So was the chocolate milk shake. The speaker was probably going to start talking about sugar next, and how evil it was.

She did.

The lecture title was "Natural Foods and the World's Shrinking Resources." It had sounded interesting, the woman was a well-known author, and I wanted to learn more about natural foods. They were everywhere—in magazines, on TV—and every week it seemed like some other additive in packaged foods was found to cause cancer. I felt like I was poisoning my family every time I made dinner. I was also aware of the starving people in the world and knew that somehow my life-style was related to the worldwide food shortage.

But this lecture didn't answer my questions. Instead I walked out with another page of depressing statistics, and the speaker's latest book.

On the way home, my depression turned to anger. I was tired of hearing about the problems. I wanted the experts to present some solutions. Weren't there practical, fun ways to conquer these dilemmas in an ordinary kitchen? I'd had experience in foods and I loved challenges. I vowed to find a way that I, as an individual housewife, could improve my family's eating habits and make some contribution to the world's food supply—no matter how small.

It took awhile. To me, natural foods meant Adele Davis, brewer's yeast, and liver tablets, unappetizing meals that might be good for me if only I could swallow them, and worst of all, the complete absence of coffee and sugar, two of my favorite things.

But I had an added incentive. God didn't bless me with robust health. For years I had been anemic, and even iron injections didn't help. My family doctor repeatedly tested me for mononucleosis because of my constant complaints that I was tired. The results were always inconclusive. Maybe natural foods would improve my health.

So I began to read everything I could. Newspapers and magazines were carrying repeated warnings about too many additives and preservatives in our food. Sugar and white flour—two household guests we modern homemakers once ushered into our kitchens—were now unwelcome visitors according to nutritional experts.

I went to work in a natural foods store and got to interact with a lot of wonderful people. I saw how natural foods worked for them. I didn't need statistical studies to learn about hyperactive children or special diets for husbands recovering from heart surgery. Nobody had to prove by test results how good foods conquered low blood-sugar problems and the multitude of ill-health complaints many people endure.

Most importantly I saw what natural foods were doing for me. Once I discovered them, I no longer had any reason to complain about my health. I had more energy then I'd had in years.

I started a natural foods cooking school in Colorado Springs, Colorado, began writing a local newspaper column on natural foods, talked on television and radio, and spoke to as many people as I could. Interested responses from hundreds of people over the last three years have convinced me that God has given me some unique and practical approaches to enjoying natural foods.

This book is the result of that conviction. In it I will share my most important discoveries with you. However, I feel that the best way to introduce you to natural foods is not by quoting statistics. I will recommend additional resources at the end of this book so you can get more factual input if you want, but my emphasis will be on the everyday use of natural foods.

I will need to begin with a framework and rationale for using natural foods, both from a personal and worldwide perspective. But after a few facts, we'll go into the kitchen and make these facts practical. Most of us already know we should be eating better. I'll demonstrate how.

Imagine cinnamon rolls hot from the oven and dripping with a honey-butter glaze, hearty homemade soup brimming with fresh vegetables, or raisin pecan pie—all these tempting dishes are nutritionally good. Eating well and feeling good is what this book's all about.

2
More Than Just a Fad

I'm not the only one who has changed my way of cooking. In case you haven't noticed, nutrition is big news. It is the latest novelty packaged by Madison Avenue and topped with granola. Nutrition has moved from little, obscure speciality stores right into the corner supermarket. Even the tiny tropical island of Kauai has as many natural food stores as it has stoplights.

A Harris poll in 1977 showed that three out of every four Americans were concerned with at least one aspect of their diet. Millions of people are thinking about the correlation between what they eat and how they feel. Some have to, because their doctors have warned them about high cholesterol and triglyceride counts and the relationship between these factors and heart attacks and strokes. Others are interested in eating right so they can stay free from disease. They want vibrant health, and they are willing to change their diets to eat in a more healthful way.

Lots of families are having the time of their lives exploring health and trying the tastes and flavors of real foods for the first time. Perrier mineral water is served instead of Coke or cocktails at some parties, and raw vegetables or fruit and cheese are nibbled instead of cheesecake. Making your own whole wheat bread is becoming a status symbol, and any cook who can't make at least one or two vegetarian main dishes is somehow made to feel deficient.

Even Congress has taken notice of nutrition. The U.S. Senate has a committee on nutrition and human needs, which came to the conclusion that Americans eat too many calories, fat, sugar, salt, and animal protein. They also found the average diet lacking in fruits, vegetables, and whole grains.

In view of this pervasive interest in natural foods, it might be interesting to see what our Creator has to say about how we care for our bodies.

In First Corinthians, Paul tells the early Christians how to live the Christian life. "Whether, then, you eat or drink or whatever you do, do all to the glory of God" (10: 31). After quoting this verse, we usually discuss all the "whatevers"—how we ought to do our jobs and house-work, etc., to the glory of God. We forget that the primary focus of the verse discusses what we are putting into our mouths. God does care about what we eat.

This is not all Corinthians has to say about our physical bodies. "Or do you not know that your body is a temple of the Holy Spirit who is in you, whom you have from God, and that you are not your own? For you have been bought with a price; therefore glorify God in your body" (1 Cor. 6: 19, 20). We are fond of quoting this verse to show how harmful smoking and drinking are to the body. But nothing affects our personal temple more on a day-by-day basis than the food we consume.

15

This verse draws an analogy between the Old Testament temple where God dwelt with men and the New Testament temple where God dwells within his redeemed people. God dedicates a large section of the Old Testament to the exacting descriptions of how Israel's temple was to be built. Only the finest materials in stones, gold, and wood went into it, fashioned by the most expert craftsmen. It doesn't seem realistic that God would not be interested in the materials that build our present-day temples, our bodies. Junk foods, fattening foods, overprocessed, and chemicalized foods aren't the best materials for the housing of God.

We are also told that we are ambassadors for Jesus Christ (2 Cor. 5:20). Nerves shaking from too much coffee, an overweight body squeezed into ever-shrinking clothes, or constant anemic tiredness isn't much of a representation of our Lord. This doesn't mean that you have to be body beautiful or Mr. America to be a good representative for Jesus Christ, but I think God will hold us accountable for the areas of our appearance that are within our control, particularly our diet and our weight. If we were honest, few of us could say we are the best caretakers of our bodies. I know I'm constantly working on a remodeling project.

But if the body is so important, why don't we hear sermons like "Dieting to the Glory of God"? I've got an idea about that, and it goes farther back in church history than you'd ever imagine.

THE BODY AS EVIL

Believers in a god who is a spirit have always had trouble knowing what to do about their physical bodies. From the ancient Greeks—who lived a disciplined, vegetarian life to liberate the soul from endless reincarnation—to those who advocate modern macrobiotics (progressive diets that are

16

supposed to help achieve enlightenment) some people have looked at the body as an evil standing between them and their unification with the divine.

The Christian church hasn't escaped this damaging influence. Though the Gnostic heresy is the best known, many errors in theology have evolved from a belief that the body is evil and must be either subjugated or destroyed or at best ignored. Much of this distortion has grown from our confusion about the ascetic life.

Asceticism came from a Greek word that originally meant "training." Christians thought of it as training the will so one would be more able to serve God. Later asceticism declined into a despising of the body, and the church rightly denied that as wrong.

Unfortunately, the church tossed out the whole concept of asceticism as well. Discipline—denying oneself for a purpose—is a badly needed virtue in our present gratification-grabbing society. The Christian ability to deny one's impulsive desires in food or whatever is an exciting alternative to giving in to every temptation.

AN IGNORED SIN

When discussing discipline in the Christian life, it is easy to forget food. We read verses like, "But put on the Lord Jesus Christ, and make no provision for the flesh in regard to *its* lust" (Rom. 13:14), and immediately equate lust with sexual immorality. The Greek language isn't that narrow; *lust* is a general term meaning "a longing, especially for what is forbidden."

I must admit that I get a lustful longing for a hot fudge sundae or cinnamon rolls fresh from the oven when I'm on a diet and such treats are forbidden. There are many other Americans like me. I suspect that one seldom hears a sermon on the sin of gluttony, because one-third of the total American population is overweight.

The Bible isn't quite so tactful. The life-style associated with gluttony in the Old Testament isn't what most Christians would want to imitate.

"And they shall say to the elders of his city, 'This son of ours is stubborn and rebellious, he will not obey us, he is a glutton and a drunkard.' Then all the men of his city shall stone him to death; so you shall remove the evil from your midst, and all Israel shall hear *of it* and fear" (Deut. 21:20, 21).

"For the heavy drinker and the glutton will come to poverty, and drowsiness will clothe *a man* with rags" (Prov. 23:21).

Gluttony is a difficult subject to talk about, because we are all guilty of it. We don't even like the term. We discuss our "weight problem," those "few extra pounds," or how "our clothes seem a bit tighter," ignoring the habit that got us into the situation. I imagine I've lost a ton of weight since I graduated from high school, and put back on about a ton and ten pounds.

It would help to face overeating honestly as the medieval church did. They called gluttony one of the seven deadly sins, and their sermons and morality plays were full of references to its consequences.

Overeating ought to be handled in the same way any other sin is. We can flee temptation, think on other things, remember the importance of our will, and encourage one another to good works. Like any other problem, we need to help each other in weight control. Nice people who would never think of offering a reformed alcoholic a drink, force rich desserts on overweight friends.

There are lots of ways to get your weight under control—groups to join, diets to try, and exercises to do. Many good books are available; the bibliography in the appendix gives a few of the books I found helpful.

Eating more naturally and healthfully can also be of great benefit. One reason people overeat is that food never satisfies them. The increased fiber in many natural foods gives the stomach a full feeling sooner and consequently cuts down on food intake. By eating natural foods, many of my cooking students have found it easy to either lose or maintain their weight.

In addition to the options already mentioned, the Bible includes another solution to overeating that ought to be considered.

THE IGNORED DISCIPLINE

A discipline that is often ignored is fasting. The Bible talks about fasting so much that it deserves closer consideration.

There are lots of books and theories about fasting, but in my opinion one of the best is Paavo O. Airola's *How to Keep Slim, Healthy, and Young with Juice Fasting.* Instead of detailing the physical benefits of fasting, such as a cleansed system, weight loss, etc., I'd like to share my family's personal experiences.

My husband, Richard, explains his view of fasting this way. "Whenever food starts getting to me, I like to fast. I get to eating like a pig and forget what I'm doing. Fasting makes you realize how little food you really need. It puts the breaks on my appetite."

Fasting isn't easy. Some of my friends tell me they don't get hungry while fasting. I always do. I think I'm going to die, or at least faint. I never have.

To me the best thing about it is that you realize you can say no to your body's desires. That sort of training seems to carry over into all of life. It is similiar to the way running expands your lung capacity and makes you capable of other sorts of exercise as well.

Fasting is also one way to identify with the people of the world, who are continually hungry. Group fasts and discussions on hunger can be educational and enlightening. There is always an aura of unreality about them, however, because you know you can eat as much as you want when it is over. The world's hungry don't have that option.

Even though you may not wish to fast for an entire day, going without one meal or cutting down on your food for a day is another way to consciously consider your own health and that of others.

God is interested in what we eat, in our stewardship (our ability to use wisely what has been given to us) and in our concern for those who have less than we do.

I pray that whatever we do might be done to his glory.

3
Natural Foods and World Hunger

Hunger is not an enjoyable topic for those of us who love food. We'd much rather think about the latest recipe or food technique than people eating what we would consider garbage and starving because they don't even get enough of that.

To be concerned about hunger doesn't mean we have to lose all interest in food, eat soybeans every other day, and fast the ones in between. But our concern should add a new dimension to our eating habits. Though food and our eating patterns remain a source of nourishment and pleasure, they can also be a vehicle for compassion.

Most of us have heard a few statistics relating to hunger. Statistics like: from one-third to one-half of the world goes to bed hungry every night; every day 10,000 people die from starvation or from diseases related to malnourishment. In

India some 25 million people are receiving only about 400 calories a day. (One third of the food intake a human being needs to survive. Many liquid diets provide around 600-900 calories a day, and some of us know how hungry you get on those.)

Statistics are enlightening but they are hard to relate to and only the beginning of the process of educating ourselves on hunger. The global problem is so complex we have to approach it as the most challenging puzzle ever made. All the pieces are necessary for us to get the total picture, and it will be an immense job to get them to fit together.

One of these pieces is agricultural production. Only a few nations on earth are able to feed themselves. Others lack the technology that would enable them to use mechanized farm implements; or perhaps they can't afford chemical fertilizers, or their land isn't suitable for food production because it is a desert or flood plane.

Population is another piece. With an increasing birthrate and declining death rate, the world is experiencing a population explosion. The human race didn't reach its first billion until 1830. But it only took 15 years to reach 4 billion in 1975.

Politics are a piece that many people ignore. Governments decide how much excess grain goes to starving nations and how much goes to countries who will use it as cattle feed. They decide on grain reserves, loans to developing nations for farm equipment, self-help programs, and direct aid.

Climate and changing weather patterns are another factor. In many ways they are the most frightening, because they cannot be predicted with certainty or controlled. The shifting weather patterns can cause drought and floods, and areas that were previously fertile can turn to wasteland. Greenland, for instance, was once really green.

The puzzle pieces proliferate. There are cultural considerations, refugee problems, economic problems, and on and on.

SOME PRACTICAL CORPORATE SOLUTIONS

When we think of helping the hungry of the world, we immediately think of giving them money. Direct aid is an excellent short-term step, and there are many secular and church-related organizations that distribute it.

Another effective method is to give to agencies that are supporting self-help programs for developing nations. To judge the most effective use of your money, write the various hunger agencies and ask them what they are doing to make nations self-sufficient.

A good way to become informed about and involved in what your government is doing is to join the organization Bread for the World. It is a citizen's lobbying group that researches hunger issues, keeps you informed on what is happening, and encourages your involvement.

As voters in a democracy we are called upon to make decisions concerning hunger. A current slogan now gaining support is "A barrel of oil for a bushel of wheat." That sounds like a good idea when we're paying over a dollar for gas, but the food shortage isn't that simple. Remember Jesus said, "If your enemy is hungry, feed him" (Rom. 12: 20).

SOME PRACTICAL PERSONAL ALTERNATIVES

Numerous writers have noted that one of the major responses to the worldwide food problem is a change in personal eating habits, usually resulting in either a strict or modified vegetarianism.

This is helpful because it takes from seven to sixteen

(depending upon whose statistics you are looking at) pounds of grain to produce one pound of meat. In a world where many people are short of the grain for subsistence living, high meat consumption by some nations doesn't seem to be the most compassionate use of grain. Frances Moore Lappe in her pioneering book, *Diet for a Small Planet,* discusses this problem in detail and shows how more than adequate and delicious meals can be made from totally nonmeat sources.

Please don't misunderstand me. I am not advocating total vegetarianism. From a Christian viewpoint, that would be difficult. The Bible does say all things are to be used for food and nothing is to be refused (1 Tim. 4:4). However, it also says: "All things are lawful, but not all things are profitable. All things are lawful, but not all things edify. Let no one seek his own *good,* but that of his neighbor" (1 Cor. 10:23, 24).

It doesn't seem profitable or edifying if my eating habits contribute to another human's starvation. Just because I give up one steak, that doesn't mean it will end up on a starving person's plate; all the other factors must fit in also. But there does seem to be an important place for personal responsibility. People starve to death one by one, and global eating habits are changed one by one. It's easy to be concerned about individuals we are close to, but a starving mass somehow loses its identity. That doesn't make the consequences of hunger less devastating on the mothers, fathers, and children.

For example, malnourishment in the early years of a child's life is likely to produce irreversible brain damage. In the town I live in, a large lawsuit was brought against a social worker for allowing some children to be so abused by their parents that they suffered irreversible brain damage from malnutrition. The townspeople felt that this was an unspeakable outrage. But we allow the same tragedy to occur continuously on a global level.

"But if someone who is supposed to be a Christian has money to live well and sees a brother in need and won't help, how can God's love be with him? Little children, let us stop just saying that we love people; let us really love them and show it by our actions" (1 John 3:17, Living Bible).

"What use is it, my brethren, if a man says he has faith, but he has no works?... If a brother or a sister is without clothing and in need of daily food, and one of you says to them, 'Go in peace, be warmed and be filled,' and yet you do not give them what is necessary for *their* body, what use is that? (James 2:14-16).

OVERFED AND UNDERNOURISHED

It seems ironic that much of the world is starving because they don't have enough to eat when many of us are slowly dying because we eat too much of the wrong things.

Eating natural foods is one solution. The U.S. Senate committee stated that Americans eat too much saturated fat; they further suggested cutting down on consumption of red meat. At the same time, they lamented the lack of fiber in our diets. A natural foods meal with a grain-centered main dish is the perfect solution and a boost to the budget besides. That may seem hard to believe if you've never tried that kind of cooking. But you will learn it is true once you've sampled a few of the dishes in the recipe section.

4
Mud Puddles around the Rainbow

Too bad the world isn't perfect. Life can be beautiful, yet at the bottom of many rainbows we often find mud puddles. Natural food is no exception.

Though there is "proof" on either side of many natural food disputes and conclusions are often based on emotional factors rather than facts, the questions are still worth discussing.

NUTRITIONAL INDIVIDUALITY

When you explore natural foods, one thing you quickly discover is the plethora of odd diets, all claiming miracles.

There are diets without meat, diets with only organic

meat, diets based on all grains, diets without wheat, diets that avoid all diary products, and diets that combine various foods in specific ways. This is apt to be confusing, especially when the diets contradict one another.

The solution is found in a new area of diet planning known as "nutritional individuality."

Many of the specialized diets work well for certain individuals. Take dairy products as an example. One book will tell you that milk is only for baby calves, that it is mucus forming, that it will cause digestive problems, etc. Another book tells you that milk is one of the best protein foods available, that it is a great nutritional booster in cooking, and a good high-protein snack. Who is right?

I think both statements can be, depending on the person involved. For instance, Amy becomes violently ill when she eats any kind of dairy product. She has a lactose intolerance, which means somewhere along the line her body lost the ability to digest milk sugars. She has to avoid milk. Catherine, her friend, loves milk and drinks huge quantities of it with meals, when she is dieting to take away hunger pangs, and to calm her nervous stomach.

Just because some foods cause some people problems doesn't mean they are bad for everyone. We need to listen to our own bodies and realize what happens when we eat certain foods. You don't need to read a book on wheat allergies to know wheat's bad for you if you feel ill every time you eat whole wheat bread.

Everyone is an individual. Be sure to choose only what's right for you.

VITAMINS

Individuals also have different vitamin needs. Ideally we ought to get all the necessary nutrients from our food if we are eating healthful, well-balanced diets. Unfortunately, I've never found anyone whose diet consistently fits that description. There are also those who are on medical diets or diets to reduce and their food intake is limited. A good vitamin and mineral supplement can be helpful for most of us.

What about the people who take huge amounts of mega-vitamins? Some specific problems do seem to be alleviated by taking larger than normal amounts of vitamins. I have seen allergies helped by vitamin C and surgery recovery speeded by vitamin E.

If you are going to take larger than normal amounts of vitamins, you ought to know more about what you're doing than just a friend's advice. *Prevention* magazine carries excellent articles and examples and explanations on the value of various vitamins. One of the best books explaining vitamins in an easy to read, helpful way is the *Nutrition Almanac*. It explains each nutrient, what it will and won't do, and what conditions it's proven helpful with. Unfortunately some people spend huge amounts of money taking large doses of vitamins, motivated solely by fear or effective advertising.

Remember that vitamins should never become a substitute for good overall nutrition. They are *supplements,* not the whole diet, and you are deceiving yourself if you think it is an improvement to rely on vitamins and protein powder and make no other dietary changes.

Be careful of the high-pressured sales tactics of some vitamin companies. I find much of it distasteful. I've heard their tapes, speeches, and promises of the abundant life through vitamins and protein powder. I see Christians, who would never intrude upon another's privacy to share Jesus Christ, hound every neighbor on the block with samples of the latest pill. Such overzealousness seems a waste of time and enthusiasm. Obviously Jesus makes more of a difference in one's life than vitamin C.

ADDITIVES

If vitamins are natural foods' knights in shining armor, chemical additives are the bogeymen. Bad as the chemical titles sound, however, the additives are not without supporters. The food industry informs us that everything is safe, and the government's warnings are reactionary. Natural food advocates respond by cautioning us against buying anything with an ingredient name we cannot pronounce.

As so often is the case, the truth lies somewhere between the two extremes. Some additives can be helpful. Salt, herbs, and spices are all additives. Some overcome undesirable properties in foods such as extreme separation of ingredients, spoilage, or food poisoning. Some add vitamins or fortification of nutrients lost in necessary processing.

Other additives are harmful. They allow food manufacturers to substitute a chemical, which may mask rather than prevent spoilage, for an expensive ingredient. Such additives may cause cancer or other diseases.

How is the consumer to know? What about the common food additives like alpha tocopherol, BHA and BHT, lecithin, and sodium nitrite?

Two of them, alpha tocopherol and lecithin are not only safe but are also sold in tablet form as food supplements. Alpha tocopherol, also known as vitamin E, is an excellent antioxident in foods, which means it keeps oils from becoming rancid. Lecithin, in addition to helping to emulsify the cholesterol in the blood and thus prevent its buildup and consequent heart attacks, also emulsifies the fats in ice cream and candy.

The other two additives, BHA and BHT, are also antioxidants, but their effectiveness has never been conclusively

29

proved. In addition they have been shown to cause unfavorable changes in the body and to accumulate in body fat.

Sodium nitrite is one of the few food additives known to have caused deaths in the United States, in addition to forming cancer-causing chemicals in the body.

For more information, *Eater's Digest: the Consumer's Factbook of Food Additives* by Michael F. Jacobson discusses food additives in detail and explains which ones are harmful and which are helpful.

NATURAL JUNK

There is no area of natural foods that the consumer must be more careful of than snacks. Since natural foods are now big business, the food industry is fond of labels that prominently display the word *natural*. Many of the new products are an honest attempt to provide more nutritious food, but unfortunately others contain only an old-fashioned label, a few token ingredients, and a bigger price tag.

Snack foods are one of the worst offenders because everybody likes goodies and we want to believe they are healthy. Label reading will reveal some disappointing facts. Just because a candy bar happens to be carob instead of chocolate, it is often still full of sugar and harmful chemicals and fat. That tiny bit of carob doesn't make it healthy. Nor is it any better if instead of white sugar it contains raw sugar, brown sugar, turbinado, or corn syrup. The effect on the body is the same.

Although it doesn't seem possible that a delicious candy can be made without sugar (in fact the word *candy* is derived from the Arabic word for sugar), it can be found. Such candy usually contains raisins, or other dried fruits; nuts or nut butter; granola; and carob as major ingredients. These candies don't taste like Hershey's and they don't attempt to.

They are a yummy and healthful product all their own.

DANGEROUS PUDDLES

In the previous chapter we discussed some reasons for cutting down on meat consumption. In addition to its relationship to world hunger, there is another reason some people cut down on their meat intake. It is called "empathetic vegetarianism."

Empathetic vegetarianism can be summed up by one of its bumper-sticker slogans: "Love animals, don't eat them." It's an idea based on the belief that all conscious life, from animals to man, shares a common existence. Since we would never eat another human being, we should not eat a fellow animal.

This idea comes from a religious view of the world that is Eastern in origin and totally antithetical to the Christian world view. Christians believe that only man of all creation was made in the image of God, only man has an eternal soul. We also believe that man was given responsible dominion over all other creatures.

The ramifications of empathetic vegetarianism enter our lives in a variety of ways. For example, if you believe that eating animal products is morally wrong, you will not use any animal products in your cooking. Perhaps you want to avoid Jell-O because of its high sugar content and a multitude of artificial colorings and flavorings, but your kids love jellied salads. You can use powdered gelatin, adding your own fruit and flavorings for just pennies a serving. If you are an empathetic vegetarian, you couldn't do that because gelatin is made from beef bones. You would buy agar-agar, a seaweed derivative that jells and is expensive.

Another food this affects is cheese. One ought to avoid highly dyed and processed cheeses. The natural food stores carry many that are undyed and natural but certain ones are labeled "rennetless," as if rennet were something unhealthy. It isn't. It is simply the enzyme that causes cheese to coagulate, but it is made from animals. If you were a total vegetarian, you would want to avoid it.

The world of natural foods can be very confusing. It is important to realize why you're choosing a certain ingredient so you aren't paying extra for something that may not morally concern you.

SOME OBSERVATIONS

An article in *Psychology Today* observed that, "Eating is seldom a purely pragmatic act done to satisfy hunger or fulfill nutritional needs. The simple act of taking food is surrounded by concentric circles of emotional, social, and mystical meanings. . . . Food is a symbol of care and a medium for celebration. . . . What, when, where, and why we eat are linked to our system of values and mythology."[1]

Our eating habits reflect our world view, our disciplines, and values. If our way of eating represents a way of thinking or a life-style that is inconsistent with our beliefs, we must be aware of that. I consciously eat meat periodically, because I do not want to be known as a total vegetarian. I consistently tell people not to take natural foods too seriously. I never want any of my students to be like the people one health food store owner described in this way.

"A lot of my customers want magic, mystery, and authority. They come in there like people going to Lourdes, wanting a cure for some real or imagined disease. Or they secretly think that there is some mystical something in ginseng, bee pollen, or royal jelly, like the wafer in the Mass, that will transubstantiate them and keep them young and beautiful forever. They ask us for advice and trust us as if we were nutritional priests. . . ."[2]

THE PROPER PERSPECTIVE

Let us return to the Bible to establish a proper perspective of natural foods:

"And He said to His disciples, 'For this reason I say to you, do not be anxious for *your* life, *as to* what you shall eat; not for your body, *as to* what you shall put on. For life is more than food, and the body more than clothing. . . . And do not seek what you shall eat, and what you shall drink, and do not keep worrying. For all these things the nations of the world eagerly seek; but your Father knows that you need these things. But seek for His kingdom and these things shall be added to you' " (Luke 12: 22, 23; 29-31).

"But He answered and said, 'It is written, "MAN SHALL NOT LIVE ON BREAD ALONE, BUT ON EVERY WORD THAT PROCEEDS OUT OF THE MOUTH OF GOD" ' " (Matt. 4: 4).

"For bodily discipline is only of little profit, but godliness is profitable for all things, since it holds promise for the present life and *also* for the *life* to come" (1 Tim. 4: 8).

Eating properly is significant but it isn't all of life nor is it the most important thing in life. The body is to be cared for, but this present one isn't eternal.

Keeping these facts in mind will help you avoid the excesses and sidestep the mud puddles I have mentioned.

[1] Sam Keen, "Eating our Way to Enlightenment," *Psychology Today*, vol. 12, no. 5, 1979, p. 62.

[2] Ibid.

5
Eating Together

We have been discussing theory: what we should and should not do in natural foods. Now, let's begin to get practical.

Since the success of our diet changes depends ultimately upon how well they are accepted and supported by those we live with and love, a few overall thoughts on eating with others might be helpful.

HOSPITALITY

Hospitality is an active expression of love. It means sharing your time, home, and resources. It is giving the best of yourself to your guests.

Think for a moment about what you are sharing with

them. You'd never think of offering someone a beer if you knew they didn't drink or forcing upon someone a cigarette when you know that smoking is dangerous to health. Yet studies on the dangers of sugar consumption and poor nutrition have shown sugar to be even more harmful than smoking. The gooey cake we baked as an expression of love is in reality a destructive gesture. Food isn't the most important aspect of entertaining anyway. People are.

Expensive food and special dinners are nice occasionally, but scrambled eggs shared with friends are much better than prime rib by yourself. Sometimes simple meals are the healthiest and often the least expensive. The recipe section will give you lots of general menu ideas to illustrate this principle. I've shared almost every dish with friends—many of whom "aren't into natural foods"—and they've all been enjoyed. As I was entertaining them, I knew I was building up and not destroying their health.

PARTY MENUS

Few foods are eaten just because they are good for you. Especially at a party, nobody is worried about protein balancing. But party snacks can be fun, tasty, and nutritious.

To make these snacks healthful and delicious, a few basics should be kept in mind.

First of all, try to think of nonsweet snacks. If your basic ingredients are nutritious instead of sugary, the end result will be health building. Think of goodies whose basic ingredients include whole grains and nuts (like the snack breads on pp. 93 and 94) or cheeses and fruits (the yogurt fondue on p. 151 or the freezer cheesecake, p. 153).

Second, think of food that can serve as meal items and not just as a dessert. Many people who attend parties have not eaten dinner, and the effect of sugary desserts on an empty stomach can be devastating. Cold vegetable platters and dips, boards of an assortment of cheeses and fruits, bowls of nuts and seeds are all good choices. Buffets of an assortment of homemade soups and breads work well when heartier food is needed.

Finally remember that a lot of a delicious, healthy food is much more satisfying than a tiny bit of an expensive, sweet one. A sugary, fancy little cake per person isn't nearly as much fun to eat as huge bowls of peanuts in the shell or popcorn.

HOLIDAYS AND OTHER SPECIAL OCCASIONS

Holidays can be disquieting even though they are often the best times of the year. We worry about gifts, about parties we have to give and attend, about whether the relatives will come and if they'll be on time. We worry about the calories we'll ingest between Thanksgiving and New Year's. We dread stepping on the scales January 2, realizing the lovely new clothes we received for Christmas won't fit until we go through a month of dieting.

Holidays are fun, and it's important to have times of feasting and celebration. One of the saddest things about the American diet and way of life is that nothing seems special. Thanksgiving turkey doesn't seem like much of a feast if you are used to steak every night. But if you have been trying to simplify your life-style and diet, you'll rediscover the anticipation of special indulgences on holidays.

CHRISTMAS

Christmas presents two problems if you are concerned about diet and health. The first is what to do about making goodies and giving them for gifts. The second concerns what to serve at Christmas feasts.

Instead of a batch of cookies to take to beloved friends as a Christmas gift, consider Christmas breads. Delicious and fragrant, filled with nuts, dried fruits, and sweet spices, Christmas breads are one of the oldest and most delightful traditions of the holiday season. Not only are they a nutritious alternative to some of the less healthful snacks eaten at that time, but when the commercialism of Christmas threatens to envelop us, breads can remind us of Jesus, who is called the bread of life. Acceptance of him means potential satisfaction of every hunger in our lives.

Another nice thing about bread is that taking time out to make it during this busy time can be a relaxing and almost therapeutic experience.

The Christmas braided loaf in the recipe section (p. 99) was especially created for gift giving but any of the other breads are nice also. Sometimes if everyone else is giving sweet dessert breads, a cheese onion loaf or a caraway bread to go with winter soups is very much appreciated.

Granola is another healthy and delicious gift. Children can help to make it for their friends, and it's fun to decide on the various flavors from maple-nut, to banana chip, to peanut butter (p.88).

Put the finished product into clear bags and tie with a big bow. Granola can also be made up weeks ahead of time.

Instead of setting out candy and cookies when friends drop in, a Christmas tradition at our house is to have big bowls of unshelled nuts and peanuts for guests to help themselves.

One alternative to the huge Christmas day dinner is a Christmas brunch. After opening all the gifts on Christmas morning, our family feasts on a variety of homemade quiches (p. 132), Christmas breads, cinnamon rolls, and coffee cakes (pp. 98-101), and a huge fruit compote. Juices, coffee, and teas complete this holiday feast.

HALLOWEEN

For the parent concerned about their child's health, Halloween is a nightmare. It is so much fun for kids to go out trick or treating, but the sweets they bring home are enough to damage a full set of baby teeth.

One suggestion that unfortunately involves lots of work is to contact the parents of your children's friends and suggest that all of you give out healthy treats. Then just take the kids to the houses you know. This is also an excellent means of protecting your child from the pranks played on unsuspecting children each year.

If you can't redo things on a large scale, you can give out healthy snacks yourself. Many of the ideas listed in the snacks and dessert section will work well, and so does popcorn, nuts, and fruits. Package the food in small plastic bags and secure it with a rubber band or ribbon. This not only keeps the food together but allows you to enclose a small piece of paper with your name and phone number on it so parents can call you if they are concerned about where the food comes from. It's tragic that someone can be concerned enough to make a homemade goodie or give out fruit, and then equally concerned parents take it from their children because they are afraid of what it contains.

VALENTINE'S DAY

There are other ways to express love on Valentine's Day besides the lace-and-foil hearts, bursting with sugar-filled delights.

If you still want to give a food item, consider a basket of

exotic fruits or an assortment of herb teas or little bags of natural nuts. Plants that continue to live and grow are nice. Sometimes one rose can mean more than a dozen. Or give an exquisite silk flower and add a blossom each Valentine's day as a tradition.

A note can also be a special gift. Tell the person you love how much they mean to you, recall the memories you've shared, and the growing you can look forward to together.

WEDDINGS AND SHOWERS

For the wedding itself it is sometimes hard to get away from the big white cake, nuts, and sugar mints, especially if it's a large wedding and funds are limited.

Carrot cake and natural snacks are lovely for a wedding, but the cost of carrot-cake ingredients can be prohibitive for a large wedding.

If the wedding is smaller, I have seen some lovely things done with small, homemade carrot cakes and buffets serving fruits and cheese or an assortment of quiches and salads.

For showers nothing is nicer than a large fruit compote, batter and other sweet breads (p. 93), nuts, and as a punch, any type of fruit juice mixed with mineral water.

GROUP EATING SITUATIONS

Educating children nutritionally is not easy. Of the foods advertised on TV, 70 percent are not nourishing. Most children's food habits are formed by the age of three, and if their parents do not eat healthful foods, the children will not be likely to want them. The problem is increased when the child enters school; many schools' food programs consist of tasteless, nutritionally poor products. When parents be come concerned about better nutrition and sincerely try to develop better eating habits at home, it can be very frustrating to see unhealthy food served at school, scout camps, and church groups.

Sara Sloan, food services director of the Fulton County Schools in Georgia, has instituted a revolutionary program that could radically change the nutritional value of institutional cooking. She shares her wisdom in a book titled *A Guide for Nutra Lunches and Natural Foods*.

In 1966 the Fulton County Schools decided to offer a nutritional choice for students in the lunch program. At that time 64 percent of the students chose to participate. Last year the participation rate was up to 87 percent. The success of the program is high because the food is tasty, attractively prepared and presented, and because the food program is not just centered in the cafeteria.

The program seeks to totally change the students' views of nutrition. Ms. Sloan includes numerous ideas for learning projects connected with nutrition. For example, students in grade schools are taught about sprouts, and learn to sprout their own batch in little pint jars, which they can take home. Brief daily lectures by grade school teachers explain the nutritional advantages of the foods prior to lunchtime and weekly PA system addresses by the principals concerning nutrition inform high school students.

In her book Ms. Sloan moves from the idealism of theory to practical problems. Cost charts, suppliers, meal-by-meal information, and ideas on setting up the program are all included. This book is also excellent for those who work with camps, church groups, and others who do any kind of institutional cooking.

Eating in a large group is an effective way to educate kids on nutrition. I could lecture the kids I worked with all day long about nutrition—how delicious whole grains and fiber are for the body, about their need for fresh vegetables and fruits—and not make one dent in their diets. But when I had them as a captive audience at a weekend camp and they were served homemade soup, whole wheat bread, and healthful green salads, their enjoyment of this food made healthful eating more acceptable to them.

ENCOURAGING ONE ANOTHER TO GOOD FOODS

An interesting thing has happened in my cooking classes. One lady will take the class; then all her friends sign up. Once a dental hygienist took some classes, and soon I had lots of people attending who worked for dentists. I've had neighborhoods, offices, and church groups take the classes together.

I think that's great. When you change your eating habits with your friends, you encourage one another. You don't have to worry about explaining when you entertain; you can try dishes together and find answers to problems. It becomes a shared hobby instead of a personal crusade.

One church learns about natural foods in their AGAPE group. No, it's not a Bible study or music group. In this case AGAPE means "A Group Appreciating Particular Edibles." They get together once a month for a natural foods meal and maybe listen to a tape or have someone talk about nutrition. But mostly they spend their time enjoying the food and each other.

Eating together can be fun and nutritious. Entertain with natural foods sometime and see what happens.

6
Eating Suggestions for Special People

Many cookbooks and diets seem planned for a family of four: two adults and two young children. The majority of life is not spent that way, so let's consider some other circumstances.

BABYHOOD AND CHILDHOOD

I was having lunch with a very dear friend one day, and we were discussing his newfound interest in natural foods. As he talked I realized how much an earlier change in his eating habits would have meant to this good-looking, slender man in his late twenties.

"Now that I'm becoming involved in natural foods," he said, "I understand some of the problems I had as a child. My diet was almost all refined carbohydrates, sugars, and starches—desserts and goodies. I wouldn't eat vegetables. My rule was: don't eat anything if it's green. I wouldn't even eat green jelly beans. I was very overweight and had terrible acne. Now I understand why.

"You can solve the dietary problems," he continued. "But no matter what I do to my diet today, it'll never erase the emotional scars my health and diet caused me as a child."

I'd never thought of it that way before.

Many people are aware of the problems of hyperactivity in children and how this has been linked with diet. We know that too many sweets cause cavities. If a child isn't eating his fruits and vegetables, the lack of vitamins can cause colds. All of these are valid concerns. But the emotional pain and scarring of a child in poor health didn't occur to me until I talked to my friend.

Little kids often aren't tactful or kind. If a child is overweight, he's called "fatty." If he can't participate in sports because of low blood sugar or asthma, he's a "sissy." If he's hyperactive, he is a "troublemaker," or he's quietly sedated. The responsibility of proper nutrition for children cannot be overestimated.

There isn't a more important time for good nutrition than during a child's formative years. Parents are not only providing correct foods for growing bodies, they are also implanting attitudes toward foods. Mom won't always be around when the candy bar is offered in trade for an apple, but even a small child can learn to take responsibility for his eating habits.

One evening, Carla, a friend and one of my cooking-class students, told us the story of her small daughter's intelligence test for kindergarten. The child was to fill in the blanks in the teacher's statements. For example, the teacher would say, "Snow is white and grass is _____." The child was to say "green."

EATING NATURALLY

Little Cindy nodded her head and the test proceeded.
"Lemons are sour," the teacher said, "and sugar is ___."
"Bad!" was Cindy's immediate response.

The teacher looked at her a moment and said, "That's right!"

Her mother, having heard the story from the teacher, was justifiably proud as she shared it with us.

Childhood is the easiest time to inculcate good nutritional habits before bad ones form. If the child is still a baby, there are good books on how to prepare baby foods without exposing your child to the heavily sugared, salted, and overpriced prepared foods.

Eating decisions are often a child's only expression of control over his life. If he or she is involved in those decisions, the child is bound to go along with them easier. When children are old enough to read, make them the label scanners. Have them choose the healthiest snacks or the ingredients for salads or granola. Have them shape the whole wheat rolls. If children are given fruits or special breads instead of rich desserts for treats, then sweets won't assume such an importance in their lives.

SUGGESTIONS ON INTERESTING KIDS

God has given us a circle of people to care for. Many of us are responsible for teenagers and should see to it that their diets are appealing and nutritious.

For example, my husband and I sponsor a youth group at our church. I have always tried to interest "my kids" in healthy eating. I took some ribbing as I prepared whole wheat bread and granola for retreats or gave natural food pep talks. At times, I wondered if it was worth it. Did they eat what I gave them just to be polite? Did they care or even notice?

One day I got my answer. Instead of making a healthy snack, such as carrot cake or homemade ice cream, after one Bible study, I bought soda and sugar cookies. Jim, a 6'4" basketball player, poked around at the food, then mumbled, "What's the deal? Don't you love us anymore?" I felt awful, but became even more determined to find ways to prepare healthy, appetizing food for the people I love.

Still, I used to be awful. When someone would ask me how to involve their children in natural cooking, instead of being helpful, I'd say, "I'm trying to get thirty teenagers in our young people's group involved in natural foods, and you think you have problems!"

Fortunately some of my cooking-class students shared much more helpful ideas, which I will pass on to you:

• "Have young people help make some of the foods, like their own natural candies."

• "With teenagers stress how good foods improve their skin, weight, and athletic performance. Who could turn that down?"

• "Start with healthy snacks for kids; then on to other foods."

OLDER EATING HABITS

We're all aware of the importance of good nutrition for babies, and a perennial part of rearing small children involves getting them to eat vegetables and other nonintrinsically tasty items that are "good for them." The teenage years are still a constant fight to fend off junk foods, and the first move into one's own apartment often finds a pantry stocked with pop, breakfast bars, peanut butter, and canned soup.

Somehow when we reach that nebulous area of "middle age," nutrition tends to be forgotten and we drink lots of coffee to keep going. This is unfortunate because throughout our lives—not just when one is young and growing—what we eat determines our health and quality of life. The body is not a static organism. It is either growing and repairing itself or degenerating, either with minor complaints or major illnesses. The option is determined largely by what we put into our mouths.

One of the most common dietary changes we need to make when we grow older involves the "middle-aged bulge." The weight gain isn't an occupational hazard of growing older but the result of continuing to consume calories in the same amounts we did when we were younger and more active. One's metabolism slows with maturity, and compounded with less activity, the pounds build up. Statistically we need about 20 percent fewer calories at age sixty-five than we do at age twenty. That means smaller portions and less snacking to maintain a proper weight.

This decrease in caloric needs makes things a bit tricky because the need for essential nutrients other than calories remains much the same. It is especially important, therefore, to get the most from one's food by eating grains, fruits, vegetables, dairy products, and lean meats and to avoid as much as possible sweets and junk food that supply calories and little else.

Special dietary supplementation may also be required. For example, the older we get, our diet tends to become low in calcium because we do not drink milk. Either our taste for milk has diminished or our body is unable to metabolize the lactose sugar found in milk. Calcium supplements may then be used to correct this deficiency and help prevent brittle bones with their associated breakage problems. A good multiple vitamin and mineral supplement can also be helpful.

Chewing difficulties that increase with age may also create problems. By giving up foods that are hard to chew, older people often pass up meat, fruits, and raw vegetables.

This can cause deficiencies in protein and fiber. A way to correct the protein deficiency would be to eat softer protein foods such as ground meats, fish, eggs, and yogurt or cottage cheese. For increased fiber in the diet, many grains and legumes can be cooked until soft, and fruit purees such as applesauce eaten. Fiber in the form of bran can be added to juice; it is a wonderful asset in maintaining the health of the digestive tract. Studies have shown that diverticulitis, constipation, colon cancer, and a multitude of other problems can be improved or eliminated by the use of increased fiber in the diet.

EATING ALONE

"I'm a very unskilled cook and can't be enthusiastic about preparing meals for myself. . . . I rely mainly on fresh and frozen fruits, vegetables, cottage cheese, yogurt, and 100 percent whole wheat bread. . . . Probably a book of uncomplicated recipes for middle-aged spinsters would be helpful."

For the wonderful woman who wrote me this letter, and for everyone of any age who eats and lives alone, I'd like to share a few special cooking hints:

- This woman has an excellent start, far better than existing on TV dinners, frozen pizza, and hamburgers. Keep in mind that *you,* as an individual, are important. Your personal health and well-being deserves as much care as a large family's.
- Many of my recipes adapt to eating alone because the theory behind all of them is versatility. In most cases they are also easy to cut in half.
- Though most of my recipes can be cut down, it is wise to make large quantities of items and freeze them in small

meal-sized portions. This works well even if you only have a small freezer in the refrigerator. For example, make the whole wheat bread (p. 97) and freeze it in little loaves to use one at a time. All the grain dishes and most soups freeze well and can be divided easily. Try taking one day a month to make up and freeze special foods.

- Invest in good storage equipment. Tupperware lettuce keepers make it possible for a single person to purchase a head of lettuce and keep it fresh instead of wilting a few days after purchase. The same is true for the vegetable keepers. If you are a small household, food stays fresh until you can use it.

- Purchase where you can buy foods in bulk. Unlike those who benefit because they can buy huge quantities, you will benefit because you can buy in small amounts. For example buy half a cup to one cup of items such as wheat germ and sunflower seeds, instead of buying big packages that could go bad.

- Keep only healthy snacks on hand and stick to an eating schedule. Just because you are not cooking for a family, don't eat continuously or erratically.

- Form a food fixing co-op with others who would be eating alone and live near you. For example, three nights of the week three of you might eat at one another's home. You'll all benefit by the company, and each person will only have to cook one night out of the three.

Whatever your eating environment or age, consider the effect food has on your body and plan your meals accordingly.

Part Two
Practically Speaking

7
Advice on Getting Started

Hopefully you are now excited about natural foods and dying to try some, but before you jump up from your comfortable reading chair and into the kitchen, here are a few ideas on making better eating a way of life.

First of all, realize it is a process of continuing education. You can't change or learn everything all at once.

"I get so frustrated. I get confused by the conflicting information. I'm doing a little but I have so far to go," one of my students sadly told me.

"You're doing great!" I replied. "Just think of how far you've come. Like any other life change, it takes a lot of time and learning."

Don't be impatient with yourself. Nothing worthwhile is

completed in just a little time.

TRY THESE THINGS

Take a natural foods cooking class. Almost every community school catalog has such classes. Ask at your natural foods store about cooking classes. It is fun and enlightening to see unfamiliar products prepared.

Go to lectures and talks about nutrition and natural foods. Ask questions, talk to other people about their confusions, successes, and ideas.

Read books and collect cookbooks. Subscribe to a nutritionally oriented magazine; clip newspaper ideas. Make the information gathering a hobby.

Do a Bible study on food. Get a concordance and look up every verse that mentions food. Rewrite them in your own words; look for repeating attitudes and ideas concerning food. Talk about these verses in your Bible study group and share a natural foods lunch afterwards.

Now try to set goals both for yourself and your family. As a family try a certain way of eating—for example, omit sugar for a certain period of time, perhaps two weeks. Then get together at the end of the time, talk about your experience, and evaluate it. When setting goals, do one thing at a time and be realistic about it. To say you'll never eat another cookie or drink another Coke probably can't be done. But you can decide to quit buying cases of pop at the grocery store each week and only have one as a special treat at the movies.

Thinking in extremes dooms most of us to frustration and failure. I know I'll never eat perfectly, but I try to keep things balanced. A baker at a wonderful pastry shop here in Colorado Springs gave me an interesting perspective. One day we were talking. He knew I was involved with natural foods, but I have also been known to purchase things from his shop upon occasion.

"The way I like to think of these things," he said, "is that they are luxury foods, not for every day but for special times in life."

I like that idea. It's something I can live with.

SOMETIMES IT'S HARD TO CONVINCE HUSBANDS

Wives often describe their husbands as "meat-and-potatoes men." Unfortunately men are not always as responsive to different foods as women sometimes are. Here are some suggestions from members of my classes to convince the other half—husband or wife—of your eating partnership:

● "If you start with the types of food they have always liked (like Italian) and make that a little healthier, then they accept it and you can add other things as you go along."
● "No problem if the dishes you serve taste good."
● "Don't talk a lot about it; then when he says it is good, tell a bit of interesting nutritional information—one fact at a time."
● "Tell your husband you don't want him to be a heart attack statistic."
● "Be very subtle."

A PATTERN

From the previous comments, a pattern begins to emerge. Nobody likes to eat untasty things or to be preached at. But no one can resist yummy, delicious food that also happens to be nutritious.

PRACTICALLY SPEAKING

Since the pleasure and proof is in the eating, let's consider practical ways to change your eating habits.

HOW TO BEGIN

The word *practical* means "useful, disposed to action as opposed to speculation or abstraction." It means doing something about what you read—more than occasionally eating a carton of yogurt for lunch or granola for breakfast. It is taking natural foods theory into the kitchen and modifying your total eating style.

But this doesn't mean that you have to spend your whole life in the kitchen. Sometimes we associate natural foods with making everything from scratch; not only doing your own sprouts and yogurt but grinding wheat and making bread, making your own butter and cheese, canning and freezing, and making fresh juice each day. If that's what you had to do to stay healthy, I'd die young.

Not that I'm degrading those who do these things; if you have the time and enjoy them, it is wonderful. But such zeal isn't essential.

Each person must decide how to implement better eating habits based on his or her own schedule, priorities, and responsibilities. I used to sprout my own sprouts and make my own yogurt. I don't now, because I can find good inexpensive brands at the grocery store. I still make my own bread because I've never tasted any that comes close, but I don't grind my own wheat. I don't have room for a grinder, and I can get freshly ground flour at the natural foods store. Now I only make bread once a month and freeze it. It would be fun to make every week, but I don't have the time.

Being practical in natural foods means figuring out what will work for you whether you are a single student or working man, a parent raising children alone or a woman who spends most of her day at home. You need to work out the right balance of store-purchased items, easy recipes, and storage tricks that will make the best diet for your situation.

Natural foods are fun and should be approached positively, not with an upturned nose thinking you'll have to accustom yourself to eating things that taste awful. I'm not denying that the world of natural foods contains some dishes that aren't exactly gourmet delights. My first soybean casserole was so bad my husband—who likes every kind of food—couldn't even eat it, and my dog wouldn't touch the leftovers. Things have improved immensely since then. For one thing, I never make anything out of soybeans.

It helps to remember that the same world of natural foods, which includes some of the less tasty members such as seaweed, soybeans, and nutritional yeast, also includes frozen yogurt and granola candy bars. Any new area of cooking contains some unusual foods that take a little getting used to. Most people who don't consider life bearable without coffee didn't like their first cup of it.

Before actually making the recipes it helps to become familiar with some of these new ingredients, to see how they work and why we should eat them. The next chapter will contain a basic nutritional review and ingredient explanation.

8
Basic
Nutrition

Whenever nutrition is discussed—and for most of us that began with our first home economics class—the "Basic Four Food Groups" are listed. The point is made that one needs foods from all groups daily to maintain good health. That idea is good, but from there on it seems like a confusing guide. I never could figure out how the portions required daily fit into real eating patterns. For example, what if you had a cheese-topped rice and vegetable casserole for lunch. Does the cheese count as part of the dairy requirement or part of the meat group? Is the rice a grain or protein serving? In many listings, sweets are listed under one section. Does that mean you have to eat dessert every day?

I decided to revise the plan. My nutritional guide contains eight groups, no portion sizes are given, and all of the groups aren't even food. But all are necessary every day for good health. The exact amounts of each group depend upon your individual needs and may vary throughout your lifetime.

WHOLE GRAINS AND FIBER GROUP

All that most nutritional charts require in this area would be a few slices of white bread daily. That is a waste and a distortion of a major and significant source of food. Grains comprise the entire diet for many of the world's peoples and the majority of the diet for many others.

Grains can supply all the necessary protein if balanced properly. They provide complex carbohydrates needed for energy, many vitamins, minerals, fats, and fiber. They are filling, versatile, and the least expensive food group.

This is only true for grains that have not been refined. It excludes items such as white flour, white rice, degerminated cornmeal, etc. Every grain normally consists of three parts: the outer bran layers, the germ of the grain, and the part that makes up the greatest mass, the endosperm. Refining any grain takes away the bran layers, the germ, and along with them the majority of vitamins, minerals, and all the healthful fibers. It's an almost comic process, because then the rice polishings, wheat germ, and bran are sold to vitamin companies who turn them into dietary supplements for people whose diets consist mainly of refined grains. It would be so much easier to eat the whole grain in the first place.

Included in this area are breads made with whole grains, whole grain pastas, brown rice, and any other whole grain—whole grain cereals, granolas, and cornmeal, which has not been degerminated.

PROTEIN GROUP

In most food groupings this is usually given first, and it is referred to as the meat group, which is misleading because meat is only one small part of a large group of foods supplying protein that also includes eggs, cheese, nuts, grains, and legumes. Most foods in fact supply some amount of protein.

Protein is the primary focus of this group, and it's important because it is the basic material for building and repairing bodily structures. Hormones, enzymes, and the raw materials for many necessary functions including the manufacture of antibodies for fighting infection come from protein. Protein can also be used as an energy source, but that's a wasteful use because a less expensive carbohydrate will do the job more efficiently.

Protein cannot be stored. What the body doesn't use, it either converts into fat, uses as an energy source, or excretes. Most Americans eat over twice the amount of protein per day their bodies need. That results in a lot of wasted protein.

Protein is made up of building blocks called amino acids. Eight of them are called "essential," because they must be supplied daily, at the same time and in the proper proportions. Whether a food is incomplete or complete doesn't make it better or inferior than another; it's mainly a matter of convenience and cost.

It is easy to get your protein needs met by meat, because it contains all the needed amino acids in one easy-to-prepare (though expensive) food. (But on a worldwide basis meat is scarce.)

To get your protein from a nonmeat source such as grains, dairy products, or legumes becomes a little more like assembling a bouquet or painting a picture. You have to be concerned with composition and balance. Where one food is weak in a certain amino acid, you must add a food that is high in that acid, and your body will be satisfied. That takes a little more time, effort, and the extra advice of a book like *Diet for a Small Planet*. But the returns include lower food costs, lots more fiber in the diet, reduced saturated fats, and an eating style that is part of the solution to world hunger.

DAIRY PRODUCT GROUP

This group contains all types of milk and milk products, including yogurt, cheese, kefir, cottage cheese, etc.

All members are good protein sources as well as being the primary source of calcium in the diet. These foods also contain riboflavin, phosphorus, vitamin D, and vitamin B_{12}. This is important because vitamin B_{12} is one nutrient that a grain-based diet cannot provide; supplementing grains with dairy products prevents any deficiencies in that area. Dairy products also act as excellent complements to incomplete proteins.

The cultured members of this group, kefir and yogurt, provide the additional benefits of favorable intestinal bacteria.

FRUIT GROUP

In many traditional listings, fruits and vegetables are grouped together. I prefer to separate them, because people sometimes think of them as either/or requirements when both are necessary daily.

Fruits are the primary source for vitamins A and C, and they also supply carbohydrates, fiber, and large amounts of fruit sugar. No matter where sugar comes from, too much of it is hard on the body, and though fruit is a necessary nutrient and very good for you, studies have shown too much fruit or too much fruit juice can throw the body chemistry balance completely out of line.

One fresh citrus fruit a day is an excellent way to supply

vitamin C. Orange-flavored breakfast drink that is basically sugar water doesn't count.

Fresh fruits or those frozen without sugar are the best way to eat fruit. Canned fruit should be avoided because of the high sugar content in the syrup.

VEGETABLE GROUP

Everyone should eat more vegetables. They are uniformly high in vitamins, minerals, and fiber—and low in calories. They are filling, and eating crisp vegetables cleans the teeth.

The darker the color of green and yellow in vegetables the higher the vitamin content. Keep this in mind when selecting vegetables. For example, when making a salad, you'll be far ahead nutritionally if you use spinach for your greens rather than iceberg lettuce.

Nothing beats vegetables freshly picked from the garden for taste and flavor. If you can't get them, use fresh or frozen vegetables. Avoid canned vegetables if at all possible. Even if they don't have harmful additives and additional sugar, many nutrients have been lost in processing.

FATS GROUP

This group consists of both saturated fats, such as butter, and unsaturated fats, such as corn oil, safflower, and olive oil. Fats are a highly concentrated energy; they carry the fat soluable vitamins in the body, keep hair and skin soft, and supply essential nutrients in the form of fatty acids. They should be eaten in moderation because of their high caloric content. Unrefined vegetable oils are the most healthful source of fats.

VITAMINS, MINERALS, AND ADDITIONAL NUTRITIONAL SUPPLEMENTS

Vitamins are not chemicals, and they do not have caloric value. They are important in the formation of enzymes; they regulate metabolism, aid in the building of body structures, regulate vital functions, aid in preventing and curing disease, and perform many other indispensable actions in the body. Minerals are inorganic components of foods that form body structures or act in the hormones and enzymes as body regulators.

There are numerous other nutritional supplements: wheat germ bran, nutritional yeast, protein powders, etc., that may be a needed part of the diet for certain individuals. As already explained, dietary supplementation is an individual matter requiring personal study of one's own body and needs.

EXERCISE

A nutrient is defined as something that "nourishes or promotes growth and repairs the natural wastage of organic life." No one other nutrient does that as well as exercise. Exercise isn't an option to indulge in just for fun or if we have time. It is a vital ingredient in good health, needed daily and throughout all of life.

Exercise balances out dietary excesses and keeps the body in tune so the other nutrients function to their fullest. It is a better energizer than a nap and a greater boon to the nerves than a tranquilizer.

9
Ingredients and Substitutions

Please study this chapter carefully before going on to the recipe section. I will call for certain ingredients to be used—for example, honey instead of sugar—and it is important for you to know why nutritionally and tastewise you're to use a certain item, and where you can find it.

Healthy eating begins with healthy basic ingredients. It's amazing how changing some of the staples in your pantry significantly increases the health of your family's eating.

You don't have to throw everything out immediately and start over. Be easy on yourself and your budget. As you run out of one item, replace it with a healthier one. It may not seem like much when you replace white flour with whole wheat or sugar with honey. But soon you will find you've got brown rice instead of white and safflower oil instead of

Crisco. Your snacks are natural and your kitchen has a whole new healthy look.

Watch your prepared foods as well as your staple ingredients. A large amount of sugar in the diet comes from foods like catsup, peanut butter, and crackers. There are healthful alternatives available that taste good. Think of it as a treasure hunt.

HOW TO SHOP IN A REGULAR GROCERY STORE

Organic foods, natural foods, whole foods—what does it all mean when you're standing in the aisle of a chain grocery store and feeling confused? A few simple hints to shopping in regular grocery stores may be helpful.

First of all, try to buy food that is as close as possible to its natural state—food that has gone through the minimal amount of processing needed to make it edible. For example, buy fresh green beans, not canned ones with mushroom sauce. Try to avoid foods filled with artificial colorings, flavorings, and unnecessary chemical additives.

Since processing and packaging is necessary on some foods, your most important step towards health is to become a label reader. The federal government requires that all foods, that are either enriched, fortified, or make a nutritional claim contain nutritional labeling information. The label lists not only ingredients but amounts of calories, protein, carbohydrates, fat, and vitamins. Products not making nutritional claims are also required to have their ingredients listed, unless they are a product of standard identity. If the ingredients are not listed and if for some reason you need to know them, they are often found on the packing crate or can be found out by writing to the manufacturer.

In addition to reading the ingredients, it is important to

note the order listed, because they are given in descending order according to their amount in the product. For example, you pick up what you think is a loaf of whole wheat bread; then you scan the ingredient list. The first ingredient is white flour, next sugar, then carmel coloring to make the bread appear brown. Maybe near the end, or not at all, is whole wheat flour. You have just learned that what you have in your hand is white bread dyed brown.

This is just a beginning. Shopping in the supermarket for health products takes time, especially at first. To help, there is a wonderful book titled *The Supermarket Handbook*. It tells you what to look for in the way of healthful foods and lists by brand name the more nutritious ones.

SHOPPING IN THE NATURAL FOODS STORE

If you are fortunate enough to live in an area with a natural foods store, you still need to be careful. You must read labels and be discriminating. Natural food brands vary considerably in purity, nutrition, and price. Because a product is sold in a natural foods store doesn't mean it is healthy. Some proprietors are very conscientious. They will carefully screen every item that comes in, and I have known several to take large losses if they found a product inferior or not what it claimed to be. Unfortunately there are others who cater to fad products and colorful merchandising. The responsibility is ultimately upon you, the consumer, for the choices you make.

Talk to the store people. Ask for advice and help. Ask other customers how a certain item worked for them or how it tasted. People tend to be very friendly in natural food stores and enjoy swapping recipes and hints.

Buy in very small quantities at first. We are so used to thinking in terms of meat cooking, where whatever you buy shrinks when it is cooked. Many natural food items are just the opposite, and after their expansion during cooking, what you thought was a little sack of beans or millet is enough to last a year.

Be cautious also of the specialty items such as salad dressing, breads, soups, mixes, and sauces. Though they normally are healthful and contain nutritious ingredients, they are also usually expensive. Making your own (there are lots of ideas in the recipe section) isn't very hard or time-consuming.

MAIL ORDER

Another option in purchasing natural foods is mail order. Certain items can only be purchased through the mail, and some stores will send complete lines to people who can't get things any other way. The resource list in the appendix gives names and addresses.

SUBSTITUTING HEALTHY INGREDIENTS FOR UNHEALTHY ONES

My main purpose in this section is to convince you to use natural food ingredients in the recipes that follow. In addition many cooks are interested in converting old recipes to more healthful versions, and they want instructions on how to do the substituting.

My approach to converting old recipes is very simple: don't do it. You'll only be frustrated and always comparing the more healthful version to the old. There are exceptions. But sugary, white flour chocolate chip cookies remade with carob chips, whole wheat flour, and honey just don't have the same old zing toll house cookies do. Instead of trying to

65

redo an old recipe start with a new and delicious one that is healthy from the first taste. Your family will never have anything to compare it to; it is a new and delicious creation. For example, if you want something sweet try my raisin pecan pie (p. 163). I guarantee that nobody will ask you where the sugar is.

I realize, however, that this approach won't satisfy everyone, so I will give you proportions and hints on how to substitute. You must realize that more often than not the recipes will have a different taste. Refining takes out strong flavors. Sugar doesn't have a taste; it's just sweet. Honey has a distinctive taste all its own, as does whole wheat flour. Safflower oil has a distinctive flavor; lard doesn't. Many other ingredients give an expected end result because of their texture. For example, the light and fluffy texture of many desserts comes from creaming sugar and lard or sugar and butter. Creamed honey and safflower oil won't ever be the same. The problems continue to compound so substitute at your own risk.

THE INGREDIENTS THEMSELVES

In this section I will discuss the major staples and minor pantry items with suggested healthy alternatives. Please remember there is great variation in the quality of various natural food brands. I will recommend specific brands at times; otherwise try to sample before buying. An ingredient's taste won't improve in the cooking process. If you don't like it plain, you won't like it cooked.

For example, honey should have a light delicious flavor. It should taste good on toast and in tea. Some of the "raw" honey sold is bitter and awful tasting, and anything made from it will taste bad. Brands of oil vary considerably; some have a pleasant taste, and some are strong and bitter. As in all of cooking, you ought to use the finest ingredients possible if you want good results.

SWEETENERS

Little did Marco Polo realize as he trudged across India with his precious load of a newly discovered, magical, habit-forming, and potent medicine known as sugar that someday it would become a major staple in the diet of Americans. At 120 pounds per person per year and 20 percent of each individual's caloric intake, many nutritionists are pointing to sugar as a major cause of many health problems in the United States. The diseases linked to sugar consumption as listed by Dr. John Yudkin, an English medical researcher, in his book, *Sweet and Dangerous,* are diabetes, hypoglycemia, heart disease, cancer, and the more obviously sugar-related problems of tooth decay and obesity.

Why is sugar so harmful? How does that beautiful crystal do all those horrid things to your body? Understanding exactly what sugar consists of helps to understand its effects. White table sugar is 99.9 percent sucrose. What was once the juice of either sugar cane or sugar beets at 15 percent sucrose has been clarified with lime, heated, filtered, spun, and treated with phosphoric acid until every possible nutrient has been removed. The end result is a pure and complete nonfood containing nothing but calories.

Sugar doesn't stop there. It is different from other natural sweeteners such as honey that contain vitamins, minerals, and enzymes that enable the body to digest its sweetness. When sugar is taken into the body, it robs the body of all that is needed to digest it. Depleting the body of essential B vitamins is only part of this process. At the time sugar is eaten the blood-sugar level rises quickly, giving that rush of energy associated with sugar. But it soon drops far below normal due to oversecretion of insulin by the pancreas. This can result in a condition known as low blood sugar or hypoglycemia, a problem that many Americans are afflicted with.

Not only is sugar dangerous, but it is terribly hard to avoid. Of the 120 pounds consumed annually, 70 percent or 80 pounds is consumed indirectly in manufactured foods, often in the most unlikely places. Sugar is in cereal, baby foods, canned vegetables, and salad dressing as well as the more obvious soda pop, cakes, and cookies.

Volumes have been written about the evils of sugar and one of the best, *Sugar Blues* by William Dufty, is highly entertaining and readable.

Don't be depressed thinking that you will never be able to eat a delicious piece of cake again. Fortunately sugar isn't the only sweetener. The substitutes for it are delicious and healthful. Be careful though that you don't get carried away with substituting and thinking that you can eat as much as you want. The body is not made to handle huge amounts of sweetness in any form.

You aren't going to find "raw sugar" listed as a substitute. It is legally impossible to sell real raw sugar in the United States. If you carefully notice the packaging of these products, you will find they don't actually say they are raw sugar but that the product "has the taste of raw sugar." They are usually very overpriced. In reality they are either sugar that has been refined 97 percent—not much different than 99 percent—or they are white sugar with some molasses added for coloring, which is what brown sugar is. Try using some of these instead:

HONEY: When Pooh Bear carefully hoards and protects his honeypot, he probably has no idea what a miracle of nature it is. It takes 556 bees to gather a full pound of honey, and to do this they have to fly 35,584 miles, or more than once around the world. Honey is one of man's oldest sweetening agents. It has been found in the tombs of pharaohs and is mentioned many times in the Bible.

Honey is probably the best known and one of the most delicious sugar substitutes. Many varieties are available, with clover honey being one of the lightest and best. Be sure to taste the honey before you buy it, to be certain you like the flavor plain and in cooking.

If possible, buy a brand that is uncooked and unfiltered. Cooking at high heat destroys the valuable trace minerals and enzymes you are buying the honey for. Be careful of overly runny brands that could be diluted with corn syrup. Honey is supposed to crystalize when it gets cold.

There are a few guidelines in using honey that should be kept in mind. Since it is a liquid with a strong taste, honey will never taste the same as white sugar if it is substituted in a recipe. If you are making a very light sponge cake or sugar cookie, don't even make the effort. The best substitutions with honey are strong-flavored foods such as spice cakes, fruit breads, and products made with whole unrefined grains or fresh fruits.

When converting a recipe, start by substituting one-half to three-fourths the amount of honey as sugar called for in the original recipe. Decrease your liquid by one-fourth cup and also decrease the oven temperature twenty-five degrees and cook the product a bit longer. Honey browns quickly, and if you are making a thick batter bread, you may want to lay a piece of foil over the top of the loaf during baking if it is browning too fast. Also flatten out cookies with a fork or they sometimes burn outside and are raw inside.

When using honey, one of the most helpful tricks is to heat it gently until it becomes very liquid before adding it to any other recipe. A cold glob of honey won't mix with anything. When using honey and oil, always measure the oil into the cup first, then the honey so it will not stick.

You don't need to store your honey in the refrigerator; if it's untreated it will solidify. Honey has amazing keeping qualities. Old German cooks refused to use honey unless it had aged at least one year. It keeps almost indefinitely at room temperature, so don't worry about it spoiling. If the honey does solidify, scoop some out to use as a thick spread on toast, and then set the rest in a pan of warm water where it will soon liquefy.

Baked goods made with honey will be more moist and will have good keeping qualities. They will also tend to draw moisture from the air.

MOLASSES: Molasses is the original unrefined juice from the sugar cane, rich in B vitamins, calcium, phosphorus, and iron. When it is manufactured for the juice itself, it is called unsulfured molasses and is rather mellow and taffylike in taste. Blackstrap molasses is the residue that remains after refining and is bitter.

Molasses is used more as a nutritional additive—for example stirred into milk and blender drinks for increased minerals—than as a sweetener because its flavor is so strong. It sometimes tastes good in hearty items like baked beans. Substitute in the same proportions as honey.

DATE SUGAR: This is a wonderful product and a substitute not many people are aware of. Date sugar is just ground up and pulverized dates. It is particularly useful when you need a granulated substitute for sugar, for example, to roll candies in or to put between layers of cinnamon rolls. It does not dissolve, however, so you can't use it in baking and it won't sweeten your coffee very well. It can be purchased at some health food stores but the best date sugar comes from Shield's Date Gardens, 80-225 Highway 111, Indio, CA 92201.

Date sugar is also good on cereal, sprinkled on top of any

dessert, and mixed in with fruit salads and granolas. I'll mention it frequently in the recipe section.

MAPLE SYRUP: For a distinctive and different sweet flavor, try maple syrup. Be sure you get the kind that is pure and not the maple-flavored sugar water or corn syrup that is sold. Maple syrup is too expensive to be used as an everyday substitute, but it is nice sometimes, especially in fruit dishes. Yogurt mixed with maple syrup makes a delicious fruit salad dressing, and bread cooked with it as a sweetener has a different delicious taste.

SORGHUM: If you aren't from the south, you may not be familiar with this product. It is the unrefined, cooked-down juice of the sorghum plant. It is available at health food stores and in many chain groceries in the syrup department. Sorghum's taste is somewhere between molasses and honey, and it can be substituted in recipes just the same as honey, especially bread recipes, spice cakes, etc. It has a taste similiar to brown sugar and works well in any product calling for brown sugar, such as baked beans, barbecue sauces, and nut breads. Sorghum is also good on hot cereal.

VEGETABLE OILS

Polyunsaturated has become a magical, if somewhat mis-understood, word ever since the American public became aware of the dangers of cholesterol. The polyunsaturated oils deserve their fame only if they are used in their unre-fined form, because much of their healthful properties are destroyed in processing. During processing, the oil is washed with sodium hydroxide, which removes the lecithin. It is then filtered through clay to bleach it, thus removing the minerals and some vitamins; next it is heat treated at 446° and completely deodorized, making it free of all smell, flavor, and vitamins. An optional step to refining enters when the fat is hydrogenated.

To understand why this step is harmful, one must realize that the essential fatty acids that make up the oils are arranged in long chains with open links. When these links are filled with oxygen, the oil becomes rancid. When the links are filled with hydrogen, the oil hardens. Nature intended for these to be left open so they could be used in their proper function, which is to transport the various fat soluable vitamins around the blood stream to where they are needed. This process cannot happen when the links are filled with hydrogen, as when an oil is made into shortening.

Finally having taken out the natural preservative—vitamin E—the oil is then spiced with artificial preservatives such as BHA, BHT, and propyl gallate.

Unrefined, unhydrogenated oils are available if you look for them. They are usually a darker color, and there is a cloudiness at the bottom of the jar. They will say cold-pressed on the label and should be without preservatives or additives. The oil will smell like its plant derivation when the bottle is opened. There are many brands of unrefined oil available. I think by far the finest is Arrowhead Mills, especially their olive oil, which is the lightest and best tasting I have ever tried.

Various oils are used for various kinds of cooking. Try some of these:

CORN: Great in baking and good to pop corn with. Don't use corn oil for deep frying because it foams. It is also too strong in flavor for salad dressings.

SAFFLOWER: This fantastic all-purpose oil is the highest of any oil in essential fatty acids. It is great for baking, deep frying, sautéing, salad dressings. This is the oil used most often as a substitute for lard, Crisco, and butter.

SESAME: Excellent to use for stir-frying and sautéing. Good in baking and salad dressings.

OLIVE: When I talk about olive oil, I mean only Arrowhead Mills olive oil; others will not give the same delicious results. The flavor of this oil is fantastic in Italian, Greek, and Mediterranean cooking. It makes the best salad dressings imaginable.

PEANUT OIL: The best oil to use for deep frying.

LECITHIN: Sold in oil form, it is excellent to grease things with. Put just a dab on your fingers; it is very thick and sticky and will spread on any baking utensil. The aerosol nonstick coatings are made from lecithin with a propellant added.

OTHERS: The natural food stores have many other oils you may want to try. Almond and apricot are especially good for your skin. Just smooth them on after bathing or pour into your bathwater; nothing helps dry skin more.

FLOUR

Most of us encounter flour in bread. The average person today has a hard time imagining that soft, squishy loaf of white bread fitting into the category of "the staff of life" as it is referred to in the Bible. Some industrious miller way back in Roman times found that by sifting freshly ground flour between coarsely woven cloth he was able to remove the bran and germ, leaving behind a white product. White flour then replaced natural flour.

White flour was found only on the tables of the very rich

until it came into extensive popularity with the westward movement of the pioneers. With all the life-giving elements removed, white flour lasted far longer without turning rancid and came into great demand for the long journey to the West Coast.

Unfortunately by 1941, the United States was experiencing severe outbreaks of beriberi and pellagra, two nervous diseases that are easily prevented by eating whole wheat. To cure this the United States government stepped in and, in place of the dozens of nutrients removed from whole wheat bread, required bread makers to add just enough nutrients to white flour to prevent the deficiency diseases. Enriched flour was born.

Today more and more people are extolling the values of whole wheat flours and an understanding of the wheat kernel will show us why.

The wheat kernel consists of three parts. The outer layer is the bran, the white interior is the endosperm, and a small area at the base of the kernel is the germ. When flour is refined, the bran and the germ are taken away, leaving the white starchy mass containing the majority of the wheat's protein and a little vitamin E. When the flour is bleached to make it even whiter, all the vitamin E is destroyed, plus traces of the gas used to bleach the flour remains.

The bran and the germ that have been taken away contained the majority of the vitamins and minerals of the wheat berry. The bran contains eleven B vitamins, and trace minerals such as iodine, copper, and zinc. Even more important, bran is one of the best sources of dietary fiber available. Fiber is an essential element in the diet for the prevention of serious diseases including colon cancer and for minor irritations like constipation. Fiber is very scarce in the highly refined American diet (note the number of commercials for laxatives on television if you need proof of that). The wheat germ is the home of the essential unsaturated fatty acids and of vitamin E. A few synthetic vitamins added as "enrichment" do not come close to replacing what has been taken out.

Below are various substitutes. When starting to change the eating habits of families who have only eaten white flour, try substituting just one-fourth the amount of flour with whole wheat and then increasing from there.

UNBLEACHED: It will taste the same as white but some unbleached flours in the natural food stores have the wheat germ added back in.

CORNELL MIX: In the bottom of a measuring cup, place one tablespoon each of soy flour, nonfat dry milk, and wheat germ. Then fill the cup with unbleached flour.

WHOLE WHEAT FLOUR: There are several types of whole wheat flour that will be discussed below. Normally seven-eighths of a cup is substituted for one cup of white flour, because the bran is in the flour and it is heavier.

REGULAR WHOLE WHEAT FLOUR: This is what is normally labeled as "whole wheat." It is a hard, red winter wheat and has a high gluten content. Regular whole wheat is best used in bread making and is the least expensive of whole wheat flours.

WHOLE WHEAT PASTRY FLOUR: This is called a soft wheat and has a much lower gluten content than the regular whole wheat flour. For this reason it works much better to make cakes, cookies, and other desserts. If you have had bad experience using regular whole wheat for some foods, try this.

SPRING WHEAT: If you do a lot of bread making and if this

is available, purchase some for bread making. It is higher in price but makes a delicious bread.

MISCELLANEOUS SUBSTITUTIONS

Here is a potpourri of pantry improvements. Try one at a time, and gradually you will have a complete new food inventory. Uses for these ingredients will be given in the recipe section.

CORNSTARCH: Instead of using this highly refined, virtually nutritionless product, substitute one for one arrowroot flour. It works exactly the same, but arrowroot is the pulverized root of a tropical plant that is very high in minerals.

JELL-O: Use unflavored gelatin to jell natural fruit juices. (See the recipe section for hints on how to do this.)

REFINED GRAINS SUCH AS WHITE RICE: Substitute brown rice. Be brave and try other grains such as barley, millet, and buckwheat.

NUTS: Instead of roasted and salted nuts always buy raw ones. Roasting destroys the valuable digestive enzymes and other nutrients in nuts, causes some to be very rancid, and adds too high a salt content. It also destroys their delicious natural flavor. The same holds true for seeds, such as sunflower, pumpkin, and sesame. Always buy them in their raw, unsalted state.

CHOCOLATE: Carob can be substituted one for one in the powdered form. Or for one ounce of chocolate, substitute three tablespoons carob and two tablespoons milk. In cookies or other baked goods, you can replace up to one-third a recipe's flour with carob. Be sure to use toasted carob; it tastes much better than the raw. Also be careful of carob products that contain large amounts of brown sugar.

CHEESE: Stay away from processed types and the dyed cheeses. Cheddar isn't naturally bright orange (it's made solely from milk and doesn't just spontaneously change color somewhere in the cheese making process). Buy plain, natural undyed types: jack, cheddar, swiss, goat, etc.

PEANUT BUTTER: Buy the kind that says peanuts and salt or peanuts only. The rest is basically peanut-flavored lard.

FLAVORINGS: Be sure to buy pure extracts, not the artificial flavorings or ones that are highly dyed.

CRACKERS: Purchase a whole wheat variety such as AK MAK.

FRUIT JUICE: Buy real fruit juice; if it's sweetened at all be sure it is sweetened with honey. Buy no fruit drinks or punches that are mainly sugar water that's fruit flavored.

PASTA: Purchase pasta that is made from whole grains: sesame, whole wheat, rice, spinach, etc. There are noodles, shells, elbows, spaghetti, and lasagna noodles. Try them all.

This is just a beginning. Keep in mind the general comments from the shopping section and learn as you go.

STORAGE OF NATURAL FOODS

This becomes a bit tricky when you are dealing with foods that contain no preservatives, that are bought in bulk, and don't come in tidy little cans.

For storing all the dry ingredients, I prefer glass jars. This gets the items out of the dark little paper bags, and you can see exactly how much you have.

It is very important to store any natural foods that contain oils in the refrigerator to keep the oils from becoming rancid. This includes not only your jars of unrefined oils—the safflower, olive, corn, etc.—but nuts, seeds, wheat germ, whole wheat flour if it is to be kept more than a few weeks, anything with a high oil content. Nut butters, mayonnaise, and salad dressings are also included. Tupperware, or good sealing plastic containers, are a must for keeping vegetables and sprouts really fresh.

Ask about the keeping qualities of the various natural foods when you purchase them, and expect a few things to spoil as you become used to new foods.

10
Your Cooking Environment

MAKE IT PLEASANT

When you come into your kitchen do you want to smile? Or cry? Do people naturally congregate in your kitchen to drink tea, to stand around and sit on the counters and chat? Do you enjoy working there or dread your time in it?

That feeling of pleasantness that comes from a special kitchen isn't a result of the latest equipment, cabinets, or high class decorating. It is a combination of organization, proper things in proper places, and the intangible quality that says home, love, and good food.

Kitchens that are a joy to work in usually look like kitchens—with the pots and pans hanging on racks, ingredients displayed in glass jars, and utensils on pegboards where they are easy to reach.

Make your kitchen pretty and fun to be in, not just functional. Paint it a cheerful color, or wallpaper a wall. Put up pictures, baskets, or plants, whatever you like to have around. Make it your favorite room, and your cooking will reflect your increased enjoyment.

MAKE IT PRACTICAL

The proper equipment can make a world of difference in cooking. The wrong tools or lack of them make the simplest things a frustration. For example, I once tried to teach a friend how to make bread with only a small bowl and a metal serving spoon to stir with. They were too small and unstable, and though I normally love to make bread, that experience angered and frustrated me. At home I use a large stoneware bowl and a big wooden mixing spoon, which makes bread making a joy.

The proper equipment doesn't have to be exotic; with the exception of a few items like good knives, it doesn't have to be expensive. Most of it can be purchased at a hardware store. Fancy kitchen items can be fun. They are great to ask for as gifts because they are something you can enjoy using and share with others. In the appendix I've listed some good places to order every imaginable kind of kitchen equipment if there isn't a shop near you.

Here is a list of kitchen utensils I have found useful:

A BLENDER: The one tool I couldn't live without. Get the best you can afford. A strong motor and the size that allows you to screw on little plastic storage jars is preferable. A good blender will make sauces, blender drinks, grind cheese and coffee beans, chop nuts, make peanut butter, salad dressings, and a multitude of other things.

SET OF BOWLS: I have a set of ten nested glass bowls I got

from Williams-Sonoma that are useful for everything from blending egg yolks to serving salads. Stainless steel bowls are also helpful.

BIG BOWL: You will need a large crockery bowl or enamel dishpan to make big batches of bread, granola, and carmel popcorn.

WOODEN UTENSILS: The weight and feel of wood is so pleasant to work with. An assortment is nice, but be sure you have at least one large heavy spoon.

GOOD KNIVES: These are a major lifetime investment, but they make an unbelievable difference. A good chopping knife, a general purpose paring knife, and a bread knife are the basics.

KNIFE SHARPENER: I was never able to keep my knives sharp until I discovered something called a Crock Stick. It consists of two pieces of ceramic that fit into a wooden base. You run your knife down them, and the knife is quickly razor sharp. This is quick and easy and takes no special skill (a place to order them is listed in the appendix). I had never worked with truly sharp knives until I got one. For weeks after that, I taught cooking classes with half my fingers bandaged.

GOOD STORAGE WARE: This includes the plastic and glass containers mentioned in the section on storage. A word concerning the glass storage containers. Instead of buying the fancy decorator kind, which are lovely but expensive, buy sets of canning jars. They come in a variety of sizes from the small kind used for jams and jellies to pints and quarts. Boxed in sets of one dozen, it usually costs less for one dozen of them than for one decorator jar. Since canning jars are tempered, they withstand breakage better.

OPTIONALS: There are so many other items—grinders and juicers, crock pots, microwaves, and food processors. Evaluate your needs, talk to friends, and buy these extra items only if you really need and will use them.

Invest some time in studying a book on kitchen replanning and organization. Organize and clean out cabinets and drawers. Throw out everything you don't need. Know where everything is and make it easy to get to. Put up pot racks, pegboards, and never stack things on top of each other. When you open a drawer, be able to see everything that's in it. All this may take some time and work, but the increased joy and efficiency you'll experience will make it worthwhile.

Part Three
Recipes

11
Introduction

This is where it all becomes real. I don't want to have just teased your mind with a few new ideas and statistics. I want your dinner table to be different. I want it to reflect health, lower food costs, and a compassion for the dinner tables of people everywhere.

More than the individual recipes, I want you to learn a whole new way of cooking. It's based on three principles: versatility, practicality, and fun.

Versatility is one of the most exciting aspects of natural foods. Since they are a relatively new area of cooking, one doesn't feel tied to the old traditional ways of using the products. Nor do you know exactly what to expect. Everybody has an idea of what the perfect fried chicken should taste like, and if yours doesn't measure up, you feel guilty. But who knows what fried rice is supposed to be like? Or lentil loaf? Yours has got to be the greatest because nobody can compare it to anything.

Fanny Farmer did a great disservice to the cooks of America when she instituted the use of level measurements and standardized recipes in her Boston cooking school. Gone were heaping cups and scant tablespoons. True, she did make things more consistent, but along with that came a loss of creativity and freedom. Let your creativity return when using natural foods. Try the various ingredients in a multitude of ways—add, subtract, exchange. Don't let a recipe be your dictator; you are the boss in the kitchen, the creator and inventor.

The natural result of versatility is practicality. When you realize you can be versatile and flexible, you're free to adapt recipes to what's in season and inexpensive at the grocery store, what's freshly coming up in the garden, and what's leftover and still usable. It's cooking based on people, not recipe books. I shudder to remember the times I honestly thought I couldn't make a dish if I didn't have that can of chopped black olives.

To implement this theory many of my recipes are what I call "basic recipes with variations." That means you have a basic idea of the dish you want to make, and then you vary it, based on what you have on hand, and what the season and budget permit. Maybe it isn't quite as consistent, but it is much more economical, realistic, and creative. Most of my recipes are like that. For the ones I haven't given variations for, think up some of your own.

Lastly you ought to have fun in the kitchen. I've always felt sorry for the nervous people who banish everyone from the kitchen and hustle and bustle to set out a meal.

I love to have people in my kitchen, helping and talking. It doesn't matter if they don't chop the vegetables the same size you would or if they mash the potatoes full of lumps. I tend to drop food on the floor because I start talking, swinging my knife, and forget what I'm doing. Sometimes my kitchen gets pretty messy before dinner, but the ensuing ingredient of laughter and relaxation is the best possible flavoring for your food.

Most of the following recipes are very quick and easy, but I've included some a bit fancier and harder for special occasions or when you just want to spend some extra time in the kitchen.

These recipes evolved and developed over many years from shared ideas, reading, travels, and cooking classes. The raisin pecan pie is an adaption of an old Texas favorite of my husband's family, the fettucini my recreated memory of a wonderful dinner in San Francisco, the dill cream a friend's family favorite, shared one summer when we were freezing a bushel of asparagus. I'd love to have time to share all the stories.

My cooking classes helped test the recipes, and many of the wonderful suggestions and variations are theirs.

12
Breakfast

MORNING MILK SHAKES

Quick, easy, and packed with nutrition. A great time-saver if the kids get up a little late for school or for anyone in a hurry in the morning. There is no need to skip on good health just because the time is short.

Pour into blender:
ONE CUP OF EITHER MILK OR FRUIT JUICE, could be strawberry, apple, orange, or any of the great natural combinations on the market today like boysenberry-apple, pineapple-coconut, etc.

Add:
¼ TO 1 CUP PLAIN YOGURT, being sure to use a kind that contains the live yogurt culture. Some good brands are Alta-Dena, Dannon, and Continental.

For extra vitamins, flavor, and fiber add one or more of the following:

1 BANANA
½ CUP STRAWBERRIES
½ APPLE, CHOPPED
¼ CUP BLUEBERRIES, RASPBERRIES, BOYSENBERRIES. Fresh ones are great but frozen are yummy also. Be sure to purchase the kind that are frozen without sugar. Blended into the drink while frozen, they will give it a thick and creamy texture. If you are using fresh fruit, a few ice cubes can be added to achieve the same frothy drink.

For extra nutrition add any or all of the ingredients below. These will affect taste, some in not very yummy ways, so experiment one at a time. None of them are essential, but some people like a real powerhouse of a drink in the morning, and these will do the trick:

¼ CUP POWDERED MILK
2 TABLESPOONS TO ¼ CUP WHEAT GERM
2 TABLESPOONS PROTEIN POWDER
BREWERS, OR NUTRITIONAL YEAST (Go very easy on this until your digestive system becomes used to it. If you take too much to start, you can get stomach cramps and gas. Use no more than ¼ teaspoon to begin with and gradually increase to 1 tablespoon.)
1 TABLESPOON TO ¼ CUP BRAN

GRANULAR LECITHIN, MOLASSES, HONEY, BEE POLLEN, POWDERED VITAMINS. Whatever else you'd like to try can also be put in.

GRANOLA WITH MANY VARIATIONS

There are so many ways to make granola, so many flavors and variations, you can let your imagination go wild. Use this recipe merely as a starting point. Granola is excellent not only as a breakfast cereal but as a snack and camping food. The *Nutritional Scoreboard* lists granola and milk as the most nutritious of all snack foods. Be careful, however, of some of the prepackaged "granolas." A careful reading of their labels shows that the major ingredient in many of them is brown sugar and few other nutritious ingredients.

By making your own granola, you can be very creative, it will cost less, and you can pack in the nutrition by adding your own nutritional boosters, such as soy flour, which greatly increases the protein content, milk powder, which will balance out the proteins of the grains, extra bran, wheat germ, and many other similar goodies. From apple cinnamon to peanut butter, you can also make your own varieties of flavor. Granola is an excellent gift for Christmas or any other time. A batch in a ribbon-tied, clear plastic bag is fun to make and a joy to receive.

To begin with, all granolas have as a base grain flakes, which can be either simply oat flakes or any combination you like. This is one of my favorites:

Stir together in a large bowl:

3 CUPS OAT FLAKES
½ CUP RICE FLAKES
½ CUP WHEAT FLAKES
½ CUP BARLEY FLAKES
½ CUP TRITICALE FLAKES (Triticale is a grain that is a hybrid of wheat and rye.)
½ CUP TO 1 CUP RAW SUNFLOWER SEEDS (Be sure they are raw; the salted and toasted variety will make the granola taste too salty.)
½ TO 1 CUP NUTS SUCH AS ALMONDS OR WALNUTS, CHOPPED
½ TO 1 CUP NUTRITIONAL BOOSTERS, SUCH THINGS AS:

SOY FLOUR	POWDERED MILK
SOY GRITS	PROTEIN POWDER

BRAN   NUTRITIONAL YEAST
WHEAT GERM

For every 3 ½ cups of the above mixture, combine the following mixture below and heat over low flame until honey liquefies:

⅓ CUP SAFFLOWER OIL
½ OR MORE CUP SWEETENER (can either be honey, maple syrup, or sorghum)
1 TABLESPOON FLAVORING SUCH AS VANILLA OR ALMOND
½ CUP DATE SUGAR (optional)

Mix together the heated oil, honey, and grains. Spread on several greased cookie sheets or cake pans. Don't have the granola thicker than about an inch on each cookie sheet. Bake at 325° for 10 to 20 minutes or until lightly browned. It's hard to give an exact time because it depends on how much you are making at a time and how thickly you have it spread on the cookie sheets. The most important thing in making homemade granola is do not overcook it. While it is baking, stir it around every five minutes so it will toast evenly. Take it out of the oven when it is very lightly browned. (It continues to cook for a while after it's taken out, and if you wait until it's brown enough in the oven, it will be too done.) After the granola is taken from the oven, turn out on a foil-covered counter or table to cool.

After it has cooled you may add:
1 OR MORE CUPS OF RAISINS OR OTHER DRIED FRUIT SUCH AS DATES OR APPLES

FLAVOR COMBINATIONS

- Dried apples, cashews, cinnamon, honey, and vanilla
- Almond extract, sliced almonds
- Honey, date sugar, walnuts, vanilla, and raisins
- Banana chips added to the finished granola are delicious.
- Peanut butter or any other nut butter can also be used to flavor the granola. Melt it in with the sweetener and oil, reducing the oil to ¼ cup and adding ¼ cup melted nut butter to each 3 ½ cups of flakes. If peanut butter is used, chopped peanuts can be added to the flake mixture.

HEALTHY HOT CEREALS

Sometimes in the morning nothing tastes better than hot cereal. Warm and filling, it's a breakfast that seems to stay with you.

Making your own avoids the "quick cooking" oats, farina, cream of wheat, and other similar products that have been overprocessed and often have the bran and germ removed. Though cereal grains are not complete proteins in themselves, dairy products perfectly complement the missing amino acids, so if you cook your cereal in milk, or add it on top, you will be eating an inexpensive and yet complete protein.

Below is a basic recipe for cooking any grain or flakes, and some combinations you may want to try. Be adventuresome and try others—just experiment with the proportions of water and cooking time to get the texture you like. In addition to combining various kinds of flakes and grains, you may add any kind of dried fruit or chopped nuts as they are cooking.

BASIC RECIPE FOR COOKING GRAINS

For coarse-grained cereals such as whole wheat berries , buckwheat, rice, etc., use 1 cup of water per ½ cup cereal. For the finer-grained ones such as flakes or cracked wheat use ⅓ cup of cereal per ⅓ to 1 cup of water, depending upon how runny you want the cereal. Bring the water to a boil, add a dash of salt, and then stir in the cereal gradually, being very careful to keep the water boiling while the grain is being added. Put on the lid, turn down the heat as low as it will go, and let the grains cook until the water is absorbed and the grains are done. The time will vary with the type of grain used. Flakes and cracked wheat take only 10 minutes or so, while solid grains such as wheat berries take 45 minutes to 1 hour.

CEREAL VARIATIONS
All of the combinations below only take about 10-20 minutes to cook. You can make up large batches of the dry mixture ahead of time, store them in glass jars, and they will be ready to cook whenever desired.

CRACKED WHEAT
This is one of my favorites, especially when it's topped with milk, maple syrup, and butter. In addition to being a wonderful breakfast, it tastes yummy if you're not feeling well, or served as a light supper. You will find this product sold either as cracked wheat or "bulgar wheat,"

which is cracked wheat with soy added to fortify it. Use the proportion of ¾ cup water to ⅓ cup cracked wheat, following instructions above.

APPLE FLAKES

1 CUP OAT FLAKES
1 CUP WHEAT FLAKES
1 CUP DRIED APPLES, CHOPPED (or more)
¼ CUP RAISINS
¼ CUP CHOPPED WALNUTS

ALMOND BARLEY JOY

1 CUP BARLEY FLAKES
1 CUP OAT FLAKES
¼ CUP RAISINS
½ CUP SLICED OR CHOPPED RAW ALMONDS

COCONUT CEREAL

2 CUPS OAT FLAKES
¼ CUP COCONUT FLAKES (best to use toasted flakes)
¼ CUP SUNFLOWER SEEDS
¼ CUP FINELY CHOPPED, DRIED PINEAPPLE

BANANA BREAKFAST

2 CUPS OAT FLAKES
¼ CUP OR MORE BANANA CHIPS (these are so good)
¼ CUP DATE PIECES

ADDITIONAL FORTIFICATION

Nutritional boosters such as bran, wheat germ, soy flour, soy grits, or protein powder can also be added to any of the above cereal mixtures to boost nutritional value.

TOPPINGS

All of the above cereals are delicious topped with milk, cream, or yogurt.
In place of white sugar, sweeten with date sugar, sorghum, honey, or maple syrup.

EGGS

If someone were to ask you what food contained the most perfect or most complete form of protein, what would your answer be? Steak maybe? Or milk?

The answer is usually surprising. Eggs have the protein structure that is most like the body and the one that is most easily assimilated.

They are a wonderful food and very popular in America. We consume about 60 billion eggs a year. In addition to being an excellent protein source, an egg contains all the essential vitamins except vitamin C, unsaturated and saturated fatty acids, important minerals, few carbohydrates, and only 72 calories.

Eggs can be prepared in many ways. The easiest way is to scramble them. I never could see all the fuss of making an omelet when scrambled eggs taste just the same to me. Besides, all of the delicious fillings that we associate with omelets can simply be mixed in with scrambled eggs or placed on top.

BASIC SCRAMBLED EGGS

Beat together in a bowl:

3 EGGS
¼ CUP MILK, CREAM, OR YOGURT
DASH SALT AND PEPPER

Cook egg mixture gently over low or medium heat until set in a small skillet.

VARIATIONS
Any of the ingredients below can be added to these eggs while cooking or can be piled on top just before serving:

SAUTEED MUSHROOMS
ALFALFA SPROUTS
GRATED CHEESE OF ANY KIND: PARMESAN, JACK, SWISS, MOZZARELLA, CHEDDAR
OLIVES, BOTH GREEN AND BLACK

YOGURT AND CHIVES MIXED TOGETHER
SAUTEED ONIONS OR CHOPPED GREEN ONIONS
COLD LEFTOVER VEGETABLES SUCH AS ZUCCHINI, ASPARAGUS, GREEN BEANS
TOMATO SLICES

A sweet topping can also be made. Heat together till warmed through and blended:
½ CUP FROZEN FRUIT
¼ CUP HONEY

Spoon over freshly scrambled eggs and sprinkle on chopped almonds.

HONEY, SPICE, PUMPKIN, BANANA, OR ZUCCHINI BREAD

This bread and the granola batter bread following are not only delicious served alone for breakfast or anytime as a coffee bread or snack food, but they also make a yummy breakfast sandwich when spread with cream cheese or peanut butter.

Cream together in a medium-sized mixing bowl:
2 CUPS HONEY
1 CUP SAFFLOWER OIL

Add and beat well:
3 EGGS

Mix together in a separate bowl:

3 CUPS WHOLE WHEAT FLOUR   1 TEASPOON GROUND CORIANDER
1 TEASPOON BAKING POWDER   1 TEASPOON NUTMEG
1 TEASPOON BAKING SODA   1 ½ TEASPOONS CINNAMON
1 TEASPOON SALT

Mix together dry ingredients, and egg, honey, and oil mixture.

Add:
2 ½ CUPS COOKED AND MASHED FRESH OR CANNED PUMPKIN OR
2 ½ CUPS MASHED, RIPE BANANAS OR

2 ½ CUPS SHREDDED ZUCCHINI

If desired you can also add:
½ CUP CURRANTS OR RAISINS
½ CUP CHOPPED WALNUTS OR PECANS

Grease well with lecithin two 5″ X 9″ loaf pans. Pour half the amount of batter in each. Bake at 350° for 1 hour.
Makes 2 loaves.

GRANOLA BATTER BREAD

In a small bowl stir together:
2 PACKAGES OF DRY BAKING YEAST OR 2 TABLESPOONS DRY BAKING YEAST
½ CUP WARM WATER
Allow to stand until yeast dissolves.

In another large bowl mix together:

¾ CUP VERY HOT WATER
2 TABLESPOONS SAFFLOWER OIL OR CORN OIL OR MELTED BUTTER
¼ CUP HONEY OR SORGHUM
1 TEASPOON SALT

Stir this mixture well until the salt is dissolved. Since I like to get my hands involved in any type of bread making, I usually stir this around with my hands. This also enables me to tell when the salt and honey are completely dissolved.

Add to above liquid mixture:
1 EGG, BEATEN
Add dissolved yeast and water to liquid.

In another bowl mix together:

2 ½ CUPS WHOLE WHEAT FLOUR
½ CUP SOY FLOUR
1 ½ CUPS ANY KIND OF GRANOLA
½ CUP RAISINS (optional)

Add to liquid and mix.

Grease either a 1 ½ quart round casserole if you want a round loaf or one 9″ X 5″ loaf pan. Fill with batter. Cover loosely with a dish towel and allow to rise until double. Bake at 325° for 50 minutes. If the top becomes too brown while baking, cover with aluminum foil.

13
Bread Making

INTRODUCTORY AND MISCELLANEOUS NOTES ON BREAD MAKING

Don't be afraid to make bread. It's impossible to have a total failure with bread. Even if it's heavy and hard, or crumbly and overcooked, the fragrance is still wonderful. Even the worst breads taste delicious toasted with butter and jam spread on top.

Keep in mind the purpose of kneading: to strengthen and develop the gluten strands that make the bread rise and to give a good texture. Remember, you want them to be stronger, not destroyed. Don't tear them as you knead, taking out all your frustrations on the bread. My bread recipes are not very stiff; they should be kneaded firmly but not violently. Also if you knead too hard you will have to keep adding more and more flour. Some extra flour is always added in kneading, but too much will make the bread dry and crumbly.

Bread freezes beautifully. Do not freeze dough, just the finished bread products.

Rising time varies tremendously, depending upon what area of the country you live in and the altitude. Bread making here in Colorado at over a mile high is a very speedy process. Quite different than making it in damp California at sea level, as I unfortunately discovered while teaching a class there. It's always better to have bread underrisen than overrisen if you aren't sure. If it doesn't rise enough, it may be a little heavy, but if it rises too much, it will be crumbly and fall apart. This is especially important when making sandwich bread, because it's rather difficult to spread peanut butter on crumbs. Bread has risen enough each time when it is what is called double in bulk; you can tell that if you punch it with your finger and the indentation stays.

BASIC WHOLE WHEAT BREAD WITH VARIATIONS

Mix together and set aside to dissolve:
1 CUP WARM WATER
2 TABLESPOONS OR 2 PACKAGES BAKING YEAST

In another large bowl combine:
2 CUPS VERY HOT WATER
2 ½ TEASPOONS SALT
⅓ CUP HONEY OR SORGHUM

RECIPES

½ CUP SAFFLOWER OR CORN OIL
4 EGGS

Stir together until honey and salt are dissolved. Add dissolved yeast to this mixture.

Stir in 1 cup at a time:
10 CUPS OR MORE OF WHOLE WHEAT FLOUR.

Add flour until the dough pulls away from the sides of the bowl and is firm enough to knead. It isn't necessary to get all of the flour mixed in well to begin to knead the dough. Knead for about 10 minutes. Return to cleaned and greased bowl. Allow to rise until double. Punch down. If time allows, let rise again. Punch down and shape the bread in any of the ways described below. Let rise until double and then bake at 350° for 30 to 45 minutes or until well browned. The time will vary depending upon which shape is selected. Makes 3 large or 4 medium loaves.

BREAD VARIATIONS

Each variation is made with ¼ to ⅓ of the recipe given above. Grease all pans first with liquid lecithin.

SANDWICH BREAD: Pat dough into a rectangular shape, pressing out the air bubbles. Roll up; tuck in ends. Place in bread pan that has been greased with lecithin. Let rise until just barely double. If unsure of when the bread is double have the bread under rather than overrisen. (Many people get excited about how nice the bread looks rising out of the pans, but if the bread is allowed to rise too much before it is put into the oven, the additional rising in the oven will be too much and the texture will be too coarse and crumbly to be used for sandwiches.)

Before going into the oven cut a slit across the top of the loaf. This allows the steam that builds up in the baking bread to escape. If this is not done, the top crust will lift off the bread, and a gap will be on top when the bread is cut.

RAISIN BREAD: Follow the same procedure as for sandwich bread but before rolling up the rectangle, sprinkle the dough liberally with raisins. Cinnamon could also be sprinkled on at this time.

CHALLAH: Divide the dough into three parts. Roll each piece into a thick roll about 18-inches long. Braid the pieces and tuck the ends under neatly. Allow to rise until double. Just before the bread goes into the oven, brush the loaf carefully with beaten egg and sprinkle with sesame seeds. Braided loaves can be made of any size. Individual small ones are nice for dinner parties and picnics.

CHRISTMAS BRAIDED LOAF: Use the same shaping procedure as for the challah, but before it is shaped knead into the dough:

½ CUP RAISINS
½ CUP CHOPPED NUTS SUCH AS PECANS, CASHEWS, OR WALNUTS
¼ CUP DRIED FRUIT SUCH AS APPLES, PINEAPPLE, OR DATES
1 TEASPOON CINNAMON
1 TEASPOON CORIANDER
1 TEASPOON NUTMEG
1 TEASPOON POWDERED ANISE

After loaf is baked and cooled, make a glaze by heating together until melted:
2 TABLESPOONS BUTTER
2 TABLESPOONS HONEY
Spoon over loaf and sprinkle with sliced almonds. It makes a lovely gift when wrapped in clear plastic wrap and tied with a bow.

CHEESE ONION BREAD: Knead into the dough ½ cup finely chopped onion and ½ cup grated cheese—could be cheddar, jack, or Parmesan or any combination of these. This is a good place to use leftover odds and ends of cheese. Shape into one or two round loaves. Allow to rise until double. Just before the bread goes into the oven, brush with beaten egg and cut an X in the top.

CHEESE BASIL PUFF: Use a pie tin for this one. Mix together in a small bowl:
½ CUP GRATED PARMESAN CHEESE
1 TABLESPOON CRUSHED BASIL
1 TEASPOON GARLIC POWDER
1 TEASPOON CRUSHED OREGANO

Break off pieces of the dough, shape into balls, and roll in the above mixture. Place loosely in pan. If there is any mixture left, sprinkle on top. Allow to rise until double and bake. This is excellent with spaghetti or lasagna dinners.

RECIPES

HERB LOAVES: You can make any type of herb bread just by kneading dried or fresh herbs into the dough before you shape it. One-fourth cup is a good amount to begin with. Some herbs you might try include caraway, dill, and poppy seeds.

BASIC WHOLE WHEAT ROLLS WITH VARIATIONS

Mix together and set aside to dissolve:
1 TABLESPOON OR ONE PACKAGE DRY BAKING YEAST
¼ CUP WARM WATER

In a large bowl combine:
¾ CUP VERY HOT WATER
⅓ CUP HONEY
½ CUP SAFFLOWER OIL
1 TEASPOON SALT

Stir well until salt and honey are well dissolved.

Add:
1 BEATEN EGG

Add dissolved yeast mixture to this liquid.

Add until a nonsticky dough forms:
3 TO 4 CUPS WHOLE WHEAT FLOUR

Turn dough out of bowl and knead a few minutes adding a little more flour if necessary. This dough is extremely versatile and flexible. At this time it can either be shaped, allowed to rise, and baked, or it can be chilled and shaped later. Or you can let it rise once before shaping it. Whatever method is chosen, once the dough is shaped, allow it to rise until double, then bake in a 400° oven 20 minutes or until desired shape is browned.

Makes one dozen medium-sized rolls.

SHAPING VARIATIONS
First grease baking pans with liquid lecithin.

ROLLS: Bread dough is like clay; you can shape it anyway you want. Make dinner rolls by forming little balls, rolling them in sesame or poppy seeds, and baking them on a greased cookie sheet. You can make little braided rolls or make loose knots of the dough. One thing I enjoy doing is to make animals out of the dough: turtles, octopuses, snakes, whatever I happen to think of. Children who never enjoyed whole wheat bread products will gobble down these rolls if they are given the dough and allowed to make their own creations.

CINNAMON ROLLS: Roll dough into a rectangular shape. Sprinkle liberally with date sugar, cinnamon, raisins, and nuts such as walnuts. Dot on a few pieces of butter. Roll up. Cut in ½ to 1-inch slices, place on end in a 9″ X 13″ baking pan.

COFFEE CAKE: Roll out into a rectangular shape. Sprinkle with date sugar, cinnamon, and softened dried fruit of any kind, such as apricots or dried pineapple. Add chopped nuts such as walnuts or pecans. Roll up. Form into a donut shape on a greased cookie sheet or pizza pan. Cut slices almost to the edge of the circle and turn each slice sideways so they overlap. Let rise till double. Bake. Cool slightly. Glaze with melted butter and honey; sprinkle chopped nuts on top.

BEAUTIFUL BAGELS

Bagels are wonderful. Chewy, firm, round little pieces of bread with a shape all their own. Bagels are unique in their preparation because they are first boiled and then baked. It takes a little longer to make them but they are so much fun and so tasty they are worth it.

Mix together:
½ CUP WARM WATER
2 TABLESPOONS OR TWO PACKAGES DRY BAKING YEAST

In another bowl combine:
1 ½ CUPS VERY HOT WATER
1 TABLESPOON SALT
3 TABLESPOONS HONEY
¼ CUP SAFFLOWER OIL

101

RECIPES

Stir well until salt and honey are dissolved.

Beat together in another cup and then add to the liquid mixture:
4 EGGS

Add dissolved yeast mixture to liquid and stir well.

ADD APPROXIMATELY 8 CUPS OF WHOLE WHEAT FLOUR and stir until a firm dough is formed. Knead 10 minutes, adding more flour if necessary to keep dough firm. Let dough rise until doubled. Punch down and knead a minute. Divide dough into 32 equal pieces if you want small- to-medium-sized bagels or into 24 pieces if you want large ones.

There are two ways to shape bagels. First you can take each piece and roll it out to about 7 inches long. Moisten the ends and seal them together to make a doughnut shape. Or you can form a round ball of dough, flatten it out, and punch the hole through the middle with your thumb. Either way you should end up with a doughnut-shaped piece of dough. Allow them to rise for about 15 minutes.

In a large kettle or deep pot, bring to a boil at least 2 quarts of water. Drop the bagels into the water one at a time. They will expand quite a bit in the boiling water, so be careful not to crowd them as you drop them in. Turn the bagel over and boil for two minutes. Remove with a spatula or slotted spoon and place on a greased cookie sheet.

Mix together:
1 EGG
1 TABLESPOON WATER

Brush this egg glaze over bagels carefully and bake in hot oven, 425° for 20 to 25 minutes or until the crust is golden brown.

BAGEL VARIATIONS

Many variations can be made with bagels, and the procedure is the same for all of them. Simply add any of the following ingredient combinations to the liquid mixture used in making the bagels, and then proceed as usual.

CHEESE BAGELS: Add ½ to ¾ cup grated Parmesan or Romano cheese.

ONION BAGELS: Add ½ cup finely chopped or ¼ cup dried or dehydrated onions. Allow dried onions to reconstitute a few minutes in the liquid before proceeding with the recipe.

CURRANT SPICE OR RAISIN SPICE BAGELS: This is my favorite. Add 2 teaspoons cinnamon, 1 teaspoon coriander, and ½ cup currants or raisins.

You can also experiment or make your own variations. Try adding sesame or poppy seeds, or other cheeses or spices or nuts—whatever you think you'd enjoy.

FORTIFIED FRENCH BREAD

Bread is one of the few universal foods. People in every land have their own bread in varing forms and flavors. One of the variations most familiar and loved is French bread.

French bread is distinctive for a number of reasons. It's actually a simple bread because its ingredients are few in number and it contains no milk or eggs. What makes it unique is its shape—the long narrow loaves—and its crust. The thick hard crust, which is large in proportion to the crumb of the bread, is what makes French bread so delicious. The presence of water during the baking process makes the crust thick and hard. This can be accomplished by brushing water on the loaves before and during baking, by spraying water on the loaves during baking, and by a shallow pan of water being placed in the oven during baking.

To make successful French bread, it is necessary to have French bread pans, which are usually curved and are made with two pans joining, so you can make two loaves at one time. These pans are used because the French bread dough is very soft; if you bake it on a cookie sheet, it will flatten out too much.

I couldn't bring myself to make this recipe all whole wheat, so I added soy flour and wheat germ to salve my conscience, and created a delicious bread recipe at the same time.

Stir together:
¼ CUP WARM WATER
1 PACKAGE OR 1 TABLESPOON DRY BAKING YEAST

RECIPES

In another large bowl combine:
2 CUPS VERY HOT WATER
2 TEASPOONS SALT
2 TABLESPOONS HONEY

Stir together until honey and salt are dissolved.

In another bowl combine:
5 TO 6 CUPS UNBLEACHED WHITE FLOUR
⅓ CUP SOY FLOUR
⅓ CUP WHEAT GERM

Add dissolved yeast and water to liquid mixture.

Add flour to liquid until a stiff dough is formed. Turn dough out of bowl and knead for at least 10 to 15 minutes. Return dough to greased bowl; let rise until double. Punch down and shape into either four small or two large, long narrow loaves. Place in French bread pans that have been greased and sprinkled with cornmeal. Allow to rise until double and then slash diagonally. Preheat oven to 400° and place a shallow pan of water in the bottom of the oven. If you have an electric stove, place it on the bottom rack. Before the loaves go into the oven, carefully brush them with water.

Bake 45 minutes or until the loaves are browned and hollow sounding when tapped.

Note: French bread is of course delicious with spaghetti or lasagna and it's yummy with a big pot of homemade soup. It's also good toasted with peanut butter and honey on top. Or just toasted with butter and a fresh-fruit butter covering it.

14
Sandwiches and Soups

SANDWICH SMORGASBORD

A notoriously powerful and immoral man lived in eighteenth century England: the fourth Earl of Sandwich. His chief love was gambling. In order to have the most time for this occupation, he invented a quickly prepared meal that could be eaten between two slices of bread.

This timesaver became known as the sandwich. From the gaming tables of England the sandwich has moved to the lunch boxes of school children, the brown bags of office workers, and the plates of persons interested in natural foods.

Sandwiches are an easy, timesaving, and a potentially nutritious meal, but unfortunately, along with much of the American diet, they have lost their health building value.

Imagine a typical sandwich: white bread, luncheon meat, mayonnaise, and iceburg lettuce. This will satisfy hunger, but why not go further and make your lunch health building. Instead of the usual ingredients, think of these exchanges.

For example . . .

INSTEAD OF WHITE BREAD:

Try whole wheat bread, either homemade (p. 97) or 100 percent whole wheat loaf purchased in the store. If your family isn't too excited about whole wheat bread, try another type of whole wheat product such as whole wheat bagels, pita or packet bread, whole wheat raisin bread, or whole wheat English muffins.

Or you can leave out the bread altogether and instead use a hollowed-out green pepper, zucchini, or a cucumber shell as a sandwich holder.

INSTEAD OF LUNCHEON MEAT:

Leave behind the meat by-products, preservatives, nitrates, and artificial colorings and exchange them for fillings like:

- Real peanut butter or any other kind of nut butter such as almond or cashew—any that are made with only ground-up nuts.
- A honey jam or honey fruit butter.
- Natural, unprocessed cheeses—jack, cheddar, swiss.
  Or try these combinations:
- Egg salad filling made with scrambled eggs or boiled eggs that have been chilled and chopped, a few chopped green onions, chopped nuts such as walnuts or almonds—all moistened with mayonnaise.

- Avocado slices, tomato slices, and mushroom slices garnished with mayonnaise.
- Cucumber slices, tomato slices, feta cheese, and sprouts with mayonnaise.
  *All of the above taste even better when sprinkled with herb or vegetable salt.
- Toasted bread spread with peanut butter, sliced bananas, raisins, and honey, and with cinnamon sprinkled on top.

OR TRY THESE COMBINATIONS HOT

- Place whole wheat bread on a cookie sheet and pile on alfalfa sprouts, a layer of sliced natural cheddar cheese, sliced fresh mushrooms, and very thinly sliced onions. Sprinkle on a few unsalted sunflower seeds and heat in a 350° oven until the cheese melts.
- This one is great to make for a large group of hungry people. Many times I have fixed it for a hungry youth group.

Mix together:

½ CUP GRATED CHEDDAR CHEESE
½ CUP GRATED MOZZARELLA CHEESE
½ CUP SAUTEED MUSHROOMS
2 TABLESPOONS SAUTEED CHOPPED ONIONS
DASH SALT AND PEPPER
¼ TEASPOON OREGANO, CRUSHED
¼ TEASPOON CHILI POWDER (optional or if you want just put in a dash)

Moisten with tomato paste and mix together well. Pile this mixture on top of slices of whole wheat bread, which have been placed on an ungreased cookie sheet, and heat in a 350° oven until the cheese melts. Of if you're in a hurry, place under the broiler until hot and bubbly.

Makes 8 to 10 sandwiches.

SOUPS

Recipes on how to make soup have always seemed rather silly to me. A more basic, ancient, or elemental food can hardly be found. If women and men could make healthy, nourishing soups for thousands of years with whatever happened to be available, a listing of soup ingredients, with instructions on how to throw them into a pot, seems superfluous.

Keep that in mind when making soups. They are one of the most flexible of all my recipes, which can be changed, varied, experimented with—and most of all enjoyed.

BASIC GRAIN AND BEAN WITH VEGETABLE SOUP

Using the proportions of 1 cup of grains or beans to 4 cups of water, cook any grain or bean or combination thereof until tender. Some suggestions that work well include:

LENTILS   PINTOS
BARLEY   KIDNEY BEANS
YELLOW OR GREEN SPLIT PEAS   NAVY BEANS
BLACK BEANS

In a separate frying pan, saute in safflower oil until tender any combination of vegetables using about 3 cups or more. Some vegetables that work well in soup include:

ONIONS   CARROTS
CELERY   ZUCCHINI

Add the sauteed vegetables to the cooked beans. Additional liquid can be added to the soup to make it the consistency you desire. The additional liquid can be either water, vegetable-cooking water, or a can of pureed tomatoes.

Season the soup with tamari, salt, pepper, and whatever herbs desired, such as garlic, basil, and bay.

Using the above basic plan, you can always make original inexpensive soups with whatever ingredients you happen to have on hand. This theory works out in practice in the following two soups: Minestrone Ala Yvonne and Vegetarian Split Pea Soup.

MINESTRONE ALA YVONNE

Cook until soft 1 CUP OF MIXED BEANS IN 4 CUPS OF WATER.

When beans are tender, add 2 16-OZ. CANS OF TOMATOES that have been pureed in the blender.

In another pan saute any combination of vegetables you happen to have on hand, for example ½ CUP EACH OF CHOPPED CARROTS, CELERY, ONIONS, AND ZUCCHINI.

Add an additional ½ cup each of CANNED GREEN BEANS and CANNED OR FROZEN CORN if desired.
Some broken pieces of SPAGHETTI OR ANY HEALTHY PASTA PRODUCT can be added and cooked until tender.

Just about 10 minutes before serving, ADD A DASH OF SALT AND PEPPER PLUS A TEASPOON OR MORE TO TASTE OF BASIL, MARJORAM, GARLIC POWDER, AND OREGANO.

Heat through and enjoy.

VEGETARIAN SPLIT PEA SOUP

Most people have trouble believing that a hearty soup can be made without a meat base. Try it. Minus the ham hock, it's still delicious.

Cook until tender:
2 CUPS SPLIT PEAS IN 5 CUPS WATER

Saute in a little safflower oil:
1 CUP EACH OF CHOPPED CARROTS, CELERY, AND ONIONS
½ CUP CHOPPED YELLOW SQUASH (optional)

Add cooked vegetables to cooked split peas. Add additional water if you desire a thinner soup.

Season to taste with tamari or salt and pepper.

BASIC CREAM SOUP

Melt in the bottom of soup pot:
½ CUP BUTTER

Add and stir, toasting well for several minutes:
½ CUP WHOLE WHEAT FLOUR

Add and mix well:
4 CUPS WARMED MILK. Stir until the soup begins to thicken and then add additional milk up to 3 cups or more until the desired consistency is reached.

After basic soup base is made, add any of the following vegetables to flavor the soup:
3 CUPS SAUTEED MUSHROOMS
OR 3 CUPS STEAMED AND FINELY CHOPPED ASPARAGUS, BROCCOLI, OR CAULIFLOWER

Season soup to taste with any of the following:
SALT AND PEPPER
½ CUP PARMESAN CHEESE, GRATED

COLD YOGURT SOUP

Mix well in blender:
1 ½ CUPS BUTTERMILK
1 ½ CUPS PLAIN YOGURT

Add 1 ½ cups of any of the following vegetables and puree well:
1 ½ CUPS CUCUMBER, PEELED AND CHOPPED
1 ½ CUPS ASPARAGUS THAT HAS BEEN COOKED AND CHILLED
1 ½ CUPS VERY RIPE MASHED AVOCADO

Season to taste with:
1 TABLESPOON LEMON JUICE
DASH SALT AND PEPPER

If making the soup with cucumbers, add an additional 2 tablespoons dried dillweed.

BLENDER GAZPACHO

Blend together:

2 RIPE TOMATOES	1 TEASPOON THYME
1 PEELED CUCUMBER	1 TABLESPOON TARRAGON
1 CLOVE GARLIC	1 TABLESPOON OLIVE OIL
1 TABLESPOON PARSLEY	1 TABLESPOON LEMON JUICE
1 TABLESPOON BASIL	2 CUPS OF TOMATO OR V-8 JUICE

If desired add:

1 GREEN PEPPER
DASH HOT PEPPER SAUCE

Blend all well, chill, and serve with croutons on top.

HEALTHY VEGETARIAN SOUP BASE

If you wish to be consistent about your health, it is very hard to find a good prepared soup stock. Many of the instant, canned, and bouillon products are mainly chemicals. In addition, if you want a vegetarian-based stock, it's hard to find one with a hearty flavor. The recipe below solves all the problems delectably. It was devised specifically for use in French onion soup but works well as a base for many other kinds of vegetable soups. After it is made, it can easily be frozen and used whenever and in whatever amounts needed.

Saute until soft in three tablespoons butter:
1 CHOPPED ONION
1 STICK CELERY, CHOPPED
1 CARROT, CHOPPED
½ ZUCCHINI, CHOPPED

111

Add:
4 CUPS WATER

Simmer for at least ½ hour or until the vegetables are very soft. If you have time, simmer them, and then put the mixture in the refrigerator to steep either all day or overnight.

Strain out the vegetables and add to the remaining stock:
½ CUP TAMARI (soy sauce)
SALT AND PEPPER TO TASTE

Use in any desired soup recipe. It can also be used as a light soup just as it is.

FRENCH ONION SOUP

Melt in a large skillet:
3 TABLESPOONS BUTTER

Add to it and saute until soft:
2 CLOVES GARLIC, MINCED VERY FINELY
5 MEDIUM-SIZED ONIONS, SLICED VERY THINLY (Be sure all the skin and root have been removed.)

After the onions are soft, add 11 cups of the stock Healthy Vegetarian soup base (p. 111). Allow to simmer gently while you prepare the next ingredients.

TOAST 12 SLICES OF FRENCH BREAD (p. 103) until thoroughly dried.

Grate ONE POUND OF THE BEST SWISS CHEESE YOU CAN GET.

Assemble the soup by putting the soup bowls, which must be oven proof, on a cookie sheet. Fill each bowl almost full with the stock and onions. Float 2 slices of bread on top of each and pile on grated cheese, patting it close to the sides. Place bowls in a 400° oven for about half an hour and serve immediately.
Makes 6 generous servings.

15
Salads

TOSSED SALADS

To save time in making tossed salads and to have the flexibility of being able to make a salad of any size at any time, wash and clean an assortment of vegetables. After chopping them into usable sizes, store in tight sealing plastic containers. Then you can take out the amount you need whenever you're hungry for a salad.

To make the healthiest tossed salads you need nutritious ingredients. Those vegetables that are highest in vitamin A have the darkest green or yellow color. Just by looking at iceberg lettuce you can tell that it has almost no nutrients. Try some other ingredients for truly healthful salads.

FOR SALAD GREENS TRY THE FOLLOWING:

BIBB LETTUCE	ENDIVE LETTUCE
LEAF LETTUCE	SPINACH
ROMAINE LETTUCE	CHARD

You don't have to use just one salad green at a time: use several for improved nutrition, taste, and texture.

Add any variety of chopped vegetables. You can use them raw or steam some briefly and chill for later use in salads—vegetables like zucchini, broccoli, or green beans. Salads are also a wonderful place to use cold leftover vegetables.

Try any of these:
TOMATOES
BROCCOLI
SUMMER SQUASH INCLUDING ZUCCHINI, YELLOW, OR PATTY PAN
GREEN PEPPERS
GREEN ONIONS
CAULIFLOWER
JICAMA (If you aren't familiar with this, it's a vegetable from Mexico, looks like a turnip when cut up and peeled but has a crisp, sweet, and very delicious taste.)

OTHER ADDITIONS

- Sprouts of any sort are also nice to add to salads. If your family isn't used to them, chop the sprouts before adding, and then they won't wonder where the long stringy things came from.

- Sunflower, pumpkin, sesame, and poppy seeds are all good nutritional additives for salad.
- Tofu, soybeans, or cheese cut in pieces increase the protein content of a salad.

TO MAKE SUPPER OUT OF A SALAD

To make salad a quick main dish have on hand small cans of beans—such as garbanzo and kidney—tuna and cold beets. Add to any salad, top with some cubes of cheese or grated cheese, and you have a healthy, hearty meal.

Note on making salads ahead of time:

If you have to make a large salad ahead of time, cut up all the ingredients but lettuce and place in the bottom of a large bowl with a tight sealing plastic lid. Place tomatoes in first, then other cut up vegetables, then place torn lettuce pieces on top and dry seeds or cheese on top of that. Toss just before serving. Layered this way the ingredients won't become soggy.

After mixing salad ingredients together, toss with the following salad dressings.

TOSSED SALAD DRESSING WITH VARIATIONS

Most commercial salad dressings are chemical marvels, full of artificial colorings, flavorings, and preservatives. The health food ones may not contain objectional ingredients but they tend to be very expensive. The alternative is to make your own. It's so much better that way—easier and more delicious.

BASIC HERB AND HONEY DRESSING

Put the following ingredients into a pint jar, shake or blend a few minutes and chill:

RECIPES

⅔ CUP OLIVE OIL OR SAFFLOWER OIL (Arrowhead Mills olive oil is the best tasting.)
⅓ CUP VINEGAR
2 TEASPOONS HONEY (More can be used if a sweeter dressing is desired.)
½ TEASPOON EACH GARLIC POWDER, MARJORAM, AND BASIL
DASH SALT AND PEPPER

VARIATIONS

- Instead of vinegar you can substitute either lemon or lime juice.
- ½ cup of yogurt can be added to the dressing to make it creamy.
- ½ cup tomato paste, a dash of celery salt, and 2 additional teaspoons of honey will make the dressing taste like a Russian or western dressing.
- To make a spicy vinaigrette dressing use lemon juice instead of vinegar and for the seasoning add only ¼ teaspoon dry mustard, 1 tablespoon parsley, 1 tablespoon chopped onion, 1 clove pressed garlic, and 1 teaspoon capers.
- Any combination of other herbs can also be added. Fresh ones such as basil are wonderful; dill and tarragon are also very nice.

HEALTHY JELLIED SALADS

Every now and then the popularity of a certain product makes its brand name synonymous with a whole group of products. To most people facial tissue means Kleenex, cola beverages mean Coke, little pieces of adhesive and gauze are called Band-Aids, and gelatin desserts are referred to as Jell-O. Unfortunately popularity doesn't always equal value.

Nutritionally Jell-O is one of the worst foods you can eat. It is 85 percent sugar, 10 percent gelatin, and the remaining 5 percent is artificial colorings, flavorings, and acid. Jellied salads have become as American as apple pie and a favorite staple to many families' menus, without adding one nutritional benefit.

There are alternatives to Jell-O, enabling you to enjoy a jellied salad without the harmful effects of the commercial, premade concoctions.

The first is to use the inexpensive, unflavored gelatin packages. Gelatin is a protein extracted during the boiling of bones. After its extraction,

116

it is then powdered, dried, and packaged. It has very little value nutritionally, but there is nothing bad about it. It is simply a jelling agent. One little package of gelatin has the ability to jell one pint of liquid after two hours of chilling or four hours if it contains fruits or nuts. The healthful advantages come from avoiding foods you shouldn't eat and from adding healthy fruit juices, fresh fruits, and vegetables to the jell.

Another alternative to Jell-O is found in natural food stores: agar-agar, a seaweed derivative. It is used widely in commercial foods as a thickener and emulsifier. Agar-agar contains important trace minerals in small amounts and supplies bulk to the intestinal tract because of its ability to hold liquids. It is sold instead of gelatin in health food stores primarily because it is not an animal product and strict vegetarians can eat it. I personally do not feel it is necessary to use it. It doesn't jell as well as gelatin, and it has become very expensive.

PROCEDURE FOR MAKING A BASIC JELLIED SALAD

Sprinkle over ¼ CUP COLD WATER:
1 PACKAGE GELATIN

Allow the gelatin to soak undisturbed for 3 minutes until it has absorbed the moisture and is translucent.

Heat to the boiling point:
2 CUPS OF LIQUID (water, fruit juice, stock, tomato juice, etc.)

Pour boiling liquid over gelatin and stir until dissolved.

Additional ingredients can either be added at this time or when gelatin is partially set. Some you may want to include are:
¼ TO ½ CUP YOGURT (can be blended in for a creamy gelatin)
½ CUP OR MORE COTTAGE CHEESE (can be added for increased protein)
1 CUP OR MORE OF ANY KIND OF FRUIT SUCH AS STRAWBERRIES, BANANAS, APPLES, OR ORANGES
ANY KIND OF CHOPPED NUTS, WALNUTS, AND PECANS

Note on juices: The new natural juices sweetened with honey are delicious and very healthful. Apple-strawberry is one of my favorites. These juices tend to be very strong and can be thinned to taste for use in the salads.

TO MAKE HEALTHY ASPIC
Follow basic recipe as above using as the juice either tomato juice or V-8. Add chopped green peppers, celery, and shredded carrots. A dash of hot sauce can also be added.

PASTA AND GRAIN SALADS WITH VARIATIONS

Delicious and very hearty salads can be made with any cold grain, bean, or pasta as the base.

Start with 2 or more cups of any of the following ingredients that have been cooked and then chilled:

PASTA: Try any of the healthy pastas, such as sesame noodles, spinach noodles, whole wheat or brown rice noodles, shells and elbows. Be sure to test them frequently as the cooking time for each varies, and if they are overcooked, they will become gummy.

GRAINS: Cold rice, cracked wheat, bulgar wheat are some of the most popular grains to use as a salad base.

BEANS: Almost everyone has tried kidney bean and green bean salads but try also cold lentils, garbanzo beans, pinto beans, or soybeans.

Mix with the cold grains, beans, or pasta any 2 or more cups of any combination of the following:

CHOPPED CELERY	PICKLES, SWEET OR DILL
DICED CUCUMBER	CHOPPED HARD-BOILED EGGS
SLICED RADISHES	

Moisten entire salad with either:
MAYONNAISE

118

OR VINEGAR AND OIL DRESSING with a dash of salt and pepper added.

If possible, allow salad to chill several hours before serving to allow flavors to blend.

SALAD PLATTERS

My sister hates to make salads. You'll never find any of my recipes for tossed salads, my gelatin delights, or grain concoctions at her house.

She has a wonderful alternative; before dinner she always serves a platter of fresh vegetables and a dip. It's easy, tasty, and nutritious. You can serve whatever you happen to have, and the leftovers can either be served before the next meal, cooked in fried rice, or put into soup.

The same basic idea can be used to make fruit platters as well.

VEGETABLE PLATTERS

Cut up and arrange on a plate any combination of the following raw vegetables:

CARROTS	JICAMA
CELERY	TURNIPS
SQUASH (zucchini, yellow, patty pan)	BROCCOLI
SCALLIONS OR GREEN ONIONS	

Whatever else is in season, such as snow peas or green beans fresh from the garden.

These can either be eaten as is or with a vegetable dip such as the dill cream (p. 124) or the following:

TOMATO VEGETABLE DIP

Combine:
1 CUP MAYONNAISE

RECIPES

½ CUP CATSUP
1 OR MORE TEASPOONS WORCESTERSHIRE SAUCE
SALT AND PEPPER TO TASTE

FRUIT PLATTER

Cut into pieces for dipping or leave whole:

APPLES   STRAWBERRIES
BANANAS   ANY OTHER FRUIT YOU ENJOY
ORANGE SECTIONS

Dip into a dressing suggested on p. 121.

FRUIT COMPOTE

This is so simple to do I hesitate to list it as a recipe, but it's so delicious and versatile. Since I have mentioned it frequently throughout the book, I will tell you what I mean.

Mix together a combination of any of the following fruits, cut into bite-size pieces:

APPLES   GREEN GRAPES
ORANGES   WATERMELON
BANANAS   CANTALOUPE
STRAWBERRIES   ANY OTHER FRUIT YOU ENJOY
ANY OTHER BERRY

You can also mix in fruit that has been canned without sugar, for example, I love to put in a can of home-canned peaches.

Another nice addition might be some frozen fruit. A bag of fruit frozen

120

without sugar and kept in the freezer can come in handy in a variety of ways. Some slightly frozen strawberries or raspberries can enliven an otherwise dull fruit compote.

FRUIT SALAD DRESSING

- Mayonnaise or yogurt (either plain or flavored) makes a good dressing.
- Plain yogurt can be mixed with any of the following to make delicious fruit dressings:

FRUIT JUICE SUCH AS ORANGE, GRAPE, OR STRAWBERRY
DATE SUGAR
MAPLE SYRUP
HONEY

- Any of the above sweeteners alone are good mixed with the fruit.
- Sometimes just a plain juice, like freshly squeezed orange juice, makes a nice light dressing.

GARNISHES
The following can be a crunchy addition or decoration for a fruit salad:

COCONUT, especially the large flakes available in natural food stores
RAISINS
NUTS: WALNUTS, PECANS, ALMONDS, FILBERTS
CHOPPED CELERY
BANANA CHIPS

16
Vegetables

BASIC NOTES ON COOKING VEGETABLES

Fiber, vitamins, taste, texture, flavor, color, minerals, trace elements, and low calories. What more can we ask for in a food than the abundance available in vegetables? With such bounty how unfortunate it is that many of the vitamins, minerals, and other nutrients in fresh produce never reach the bodies of the people who eat them.

This happens because the cleaning, storage, and cooking methods of most Americans destroy virtually all the nutrients in vegetables—and much of their fresh flavor. If you understand how the nutrients are destroyed, a few simple steps can be taken to prevent this.

Vitamins, minerals, and flavor in vegetables are destroyed by soaking or cooking in excess water, overcooking, excessive heat, air, light, soda, and salt.

Soaking vegetables either to clean them, freshen them, or to boil them leaches out water-soluble nutrients and flavors. If all of your cooking water is saved, the nutrients are retained, but despite the best of intentions, I've never known a cook who did this.

Vegetables should be brought home, washed very quickly, dried thoroughly, and then put into a tight-fitting plastic container in the refrigerator. They should never be peeled, if at all possible, because many of the nutrients are directly under the skin. The skins also provide an excellent source of fiber. When peeled, the surface of the vegetable is exposed to air and vitamin loss occurs.

Once a vegetable has been properly stored and cleaned, the best cooking methods are to chop the vegetable quickly just before cooking, and then to cook it briefly until tender by either steam, waterless method, stir-fry, quick broiling, or deep frying. Each of these methods protects the vegetable from the air by either steam or a quick oil coating. The initial high heat stops destructive enzyme action, and the quick cooking seals in flavor and nutrients.

Deep fat frying has been frowned upon, which is unfortunate, because if it is done properly it rapidly seals in nutrition and taste. One of the most important aspects of cooking with deep fat is to use a high-quality oil, such as unrefined safflower or peanut oil. Also the oil must be refrigerated between use, and it should not be used more than three or four times. A delicious and entertaining illustration of vegetables cooked this way is tempura (p. 133).

Soda should never be added to cooking vegetables because it immediately destroys nutrients; salt can also be detrimental if it is added too soon in the cooking process. Since salt attracts moisture if it is added initially in cooking, the juices that carry the vitamins, minerals, and flavor will be leached out into the cooking liquid. If salt is to be used at all, it should only be added at the last minute before the vegetable is served.

Stir-frying, the oriental method of quickly sautéing vegetables in a minimum of oil, is another method more cooks should explore. The vegetables are cooked until barely tender, thus retaining much of their texture and taste.

Steaming is one of the best ways to cook vegetables. The collapsible steamers that fit into any size saucepan are excellent to use. Put only a small amount of water in the bottom of the pot, place in the steamer, bring water to a boil so the steam fills the pot, drop in the vegetables, put on a lid, and cook until barely tender.

Now that you have a perfectly cooked vegetable, I'll share a recipe that is yummy to serve with them. The dill cream is great spooned over cooked green vegetables such as green beans, peas, or fresh asparagus. It makes a yummy dip for cold vegetables and can be thinned with a little milk to make a dill salad dressing. Needless to say it's an excellent dip for artichokes.

DILL CREAM

Mix together:
1 CUP PLAIN, FRESH YOGURT OR SOUR CREAM
3 TABLESPOONS FINELY CHOPPED GREEN ONIONS, TOPS INCLUDED
1 TABLESPOON DILLWEED
DASH SALT AND PEPPER

Chill overnight or at least for one hour before using to allow the flavors to blend.

POTATOES

Since much of the rest of the cookbook deals with many vegetables used in various ways, I'd like to devote the remainder of this section to a discussion of a favorite vegetable of mine: the potato.

Potatoes are a relatively new food in the diets of many parts of the world. Native to South America, the Spaniards found them eaten in large quantities and brought them to Europe. Here they became very popular because they could be easily grown in areas too cold and damp for producing grain, a fact extremely important to a chilly, overpopulated country such as Ireland.

Potatoes didn't find their way to America until the 1700s, and since then they have become a favorite staple in a multitude of forms, from hash browns to french fries.

Various diet fads have given potatoes bad publicity because of their supposed high caloric content, but in reality potatoes have only about ninety calories, which is the same amount as an orange or an apple. Potatoes are also high in vitamins and minerals. The average potato contains as much vitamin C as a glass of tomato juice and as much iron as an egg. They are relatively high in protein for a vegetable and yield a good fiber content.

Unfortunately almost all of this nutritional value can be lost if potatoes are cooked or processed incorrectly. Because potatoes darken when exposed to light, the food industry treats them with chemicals as a preventative. Most processed potato products require peeled potatoes, and to make this easier, they are soaked in a caustic lye bath. To avoid contamination from this type of treatment, simply buy inexpensive, raw potatoes.

When potatoes are boiled without their skins and then the boiling water is thrown away, a majority of the nutrients vanish down the drain. They should be boiled, steamed, or baked with their skins on, and the skins should be eaten with the potato, not only for a source of fiber but because most of the vitamins are contained just below the skin. Baking with dry heat conserves more nutrients than boiling, so it's better to soften potatoes to be deep fried by baking them with their skins on rather than preboiling them.

I think you will enjoy some of the slightly different, healthful ways to use potatoes that follow.

CREAMY CHEESY POTATOES

This is delicious! It can be used either as a side or main dish.

Bake or boil 5 large potatoes with the skins still on until they are tender.

RECIPES

New or red potatoes are very nice but any kind will do. (The potatoes can be peeled for this recipe but leaving the skins on greatly increases the nutritional and fiber content.)

Cut into cubes and mix with:

1 ½ CUPS SMALL CURD COTTAGE OR RICOTTA CHEESE
1 CUP GRATED CHEDDAR OR JACK CHEESE OR A COMBINATION OF BOTH
1 CUP PLAIN YOGURT (You can use less if you want the finished product drier.)
2 TO 4 CLOVES GARLIC, chopped very fine or better yet put through a garlic press
¼ CUP FINELY CHOPPED GREEN ONIONS
SALT AND PEPPER TO TASTE

Mix together well.

Place in a 2- to 2 ½-quart casserole. If desired, top with additional grated cheese and bake at 375° for 30-45 minutes.

VARIATIONS
- Leftover vegetables can also be added, such as green beans or peas.
- Add a can of tuna or salmon for a hearty meal.
- Finished dish looks lovely garnished with sliced boiled eggs and parsley flakes.

HONEY CANDIED SWEET POTATOES

The holidays just wouldn't be the same without baked sweet potatoes, and made with honey they are even more delicious.

Bake until tender:
5 LARGE SWEET POTATOES OR YAMS

Cut into slices and place in a baking dish.

Pour over:
¼ CUP OR MORE MELTED BUTTER
⅔ CUP OR MORE HONEY OR MAPLE SYRUP OR A COMBINATION OF BOTH.

If available sprinkle on top:
¼ CUP DATE SUGAR

Bake uncovered at 350° for 20 minutes.

POTATO SKINS

You won't believe how delicious an appetizer this is.

First bake potatoes until tender. Then cut the potato in half and hollow out. The shell can be cut in half again if desired. Deep fry the potato skins in hot oil in a deep fat fryer until brown and crisp. You can also fry the part that was scooped out. Drain and salt. Serve immediately as an appetizer with bowls of sour cream to dip skins into.

ALTERNATE METHOD: Bake potatoes in a hot 400° oven 45-60 minutes without foil; the skins will be crispy after baking. Hollow potatoes and fill with sour cream.

MISCELLANEOUS POTATO IDEAS

MASHED POTATOES: Boil potatoes with the skins still on. When very tender, remove from water and mash with the skins. Beat plain yogurt, butter, salt, and pepper into the mashed potatoes.

CUBED POTATOES: Steam potatoes until tender with skins on; then cube and mix with yogurt, butter, salt, and pepper. If possible add some fresh chopped chives.

FRIED POTATOES: Bake potatoes until tender. Have ½ inch of hot safflower oil ready in skillet. Quickly chop potatoes, add to hot oil, and stir to coat with oil. Cook, stirring occasionally, until brown and crisp. When almost done, sprinkle on top ½ cup chopped green onions or regular onions and cook together the last few minutes.

17
Meatless
Main Dishes

BASIC VEGETABLE FRIED RICE

This recipe is one of the most useful and versatile of all natural food main dishes. It's what I call the "hamburger helper of natural foods," because once you learn to do it, it's easy and inexpensive.

To make a quick dinner cook up whatever odds and ends of vegetables you happen to have on hand and add rice.

BROWN RICE COOKING INSTRUCTIONS

Bring to a boil:
3 CUPS OF WATER
Add:
1 ½ CUPS BROWN RICE
Or
1 CUP BROWN RICE AND ½ CUP SOY GRITS. This will make a complete protein and will greatly increase the protein content of the dish. The soy grits will absorb the taste of the rice. Allow the mixture to return to a boil. Place a tight-fitting lid on the rice, turn the heat down very low, and allow to cook for 40 minutes totally undisturbed. Don't lift the lid or stir the rice around. The rice cooks by forming a steam structure that cooks each individual grain, and if you disturb it, the grains will become gummy and won't cook well.

When the rice is cooked you can either use it immediately or you can freeze it in individual plastic containers or freezer bags. It only takes a few minutes to thaw in a microwave oven or in a steamer placed in a saucepan. By making up a large quantity of rice ahead of time, you always have on hand the basis for an instant healthy meal. This amount will make enough for at least two meals, so if you don't want to freeze it, cut the amount of rice and water in half—or double it if you want to freeze a lot.

VEGETABLE FRIED RICE MEAL

Thaw or prepare:
2 CUPS COOKED RICE

Saute lightly until cooked but still tender or stir-fry in a wok:
2 CUPS OF VEGETABLES. These can be any combination that you have on hand or happen to enjoy, such as mushrooms, squash, bean sprouts, onions, carrots, or celery.

When vegetables are tender stir in the rice.

The following can be added on top:
½ CUP GRATED CHEESE
¼ CUP SUNFLOWER SEEDS, UNSALTED, OR SESAME SEEDS
1 OR 2 SCRAMBLED EGGS

FRIED RICE VARIATIONS

- Shrimp, leftover bits of beef, chicken, or tuna can be added.
- Just before serving, chopped spinach or chard can be added. Cover and steam the mixture until the spinach or chard wilts. One good way to do this is to saute the chard stalks and onions, add the rice, lots of chopped chard leaves and lots of cheese, cover, and heat through.
- Use mushrooms, celery, onions, and a bit of leftover chicken, saute till tender, and then add some sauce made from:
  ¼ CUP TAMARI SAUCE (soy sauce)
  ¼ CUP PINEAPPLE JUICE (optional)
  1 TABLESPOON HONEY
  1 TEASPOON ARROWROOT FLOUR

BASIC PASTA MEAL

Pasta and a delicious vegetarian tomato sauce form the basis for many tasty, easy, and nutritious main dishes. Pasta stores well and is easy to use. It can also be nutritious if you avoid the bleached white flour products and try some of the new pastas that are made from various grains and vegetables. Sesame spaghetti is fantastic, and there are lots of other spaghetti, noodles, elbows, and pastas in every imaginable shape in whole wheat, millet, brown rice, spinach, and lots of other bases. Pasta is also a great way to introduce your family to natural foods because it is familiar and a food everybody loves.

The difficult part of making quick pasta dinners is the time required to make the sauce. I suggest making a large amount and freezing it in various sizes of plastic containers. When you come dashing home from work and want a quick dinner, all you have to do is thaw the sauce and put on the noodles.

VEGETABLE MEDLEY SPAGHETTI SAUCE

Pour into a large skillet:
¼ CUP ARROWHEAD MILLS OLIVE OIL

Saute the following in the oil until tender:
4 CUPS OF CHOPPED VEGETABLES including any of the following: zucchini or any summer squash, eggplant, mushrooms, whatever other vegetables you'd enjoy
1 CHOPPED ONION
3 OR MORE FINELY CHOPPED CLOVES OF GARLIC

Add to the vegetables and simmer over low heat until the desired thickness is obtained:
1 28 OZ. CAN TOMATO PUREE
1 DRAINED 16 OZ. CAN TOMATOES THAT HAVE BEEN CUT UP

After the sauce has reached the desired thickness, add the following spices to taste. (You should never simmer spices in with a sauce for a long time as this causes their flavor to dissipate before the sauce is finished cooking.)

1 TEASPOON MARJORAM
1 TEASPOON OREGANO
2 OR MORE TEASPOONS BASIL
1 TEASPOON SALT
¼ TEASPOON PEPPER
2 TABLESPOONS HONEY

Stir together and heat through on medium heat for about 10 minutes. Serve hot over sesame spaghetti or any unrefined cooked spaghetti or pasta.

VARIATIONS
This sauce also makes an excellent base for many vegetarian casseroles. For example, lightly steam some fresh green beans and cook a few cups

of the mixed vegetable pasta elbows. Mix the cooked pasta with the steamed vegetables, top with grated cheese, heat through, and an easy, delicious meal is ready.

Similar things can be done with any combination of vegetables and pasta that you have on hand.

QUICHE

Quiches can be eaten at any time of the day. They are one of the most versatile of foods. For breakfast they make a special treat; for brunch they are standard fare. Summer or winter they are a most delicious light entree for dinner.

Though they are often considered gourmet food, quiches are a great way to use leftovers. Bits of cheese, dairy products, odds and ends of both vegetables and meats can all disappear into a quiche, and the end result is delicious.

TO MAKE A QUICHE

Prepare by making a healthy piecrust (p. 155) and line a 9-inch pie pan with it.

In a medium-sized bowl stir together the following:

3 EGGS, BEATEN

1 CUP HALF-AND-HALF OR MILK OR SKIM MILK, the more cream the milk has the richer the quiche will be, the less cream the lower the calories

Add:

1 CUP GRATED CHEESE (This can be either Swiss, jack or cheddar, or any combination of these that you happen to have on hand. My favorite is ½ Swiss and ½ jack.)

Add:

½ CUP CHOPPED FRESH VEGETABLES such as zucchini squash or mushrooms or steamed ones such as broccoli or asparagus or leftovers

2 TABLESPOONS CHOPPED GREEN ONION

DASH OF SALT AND PEPPER

Stir mixture to blend and pour into pie shell. Bake in a preheated 375° oven 35-40 minutes or until the top is golden brown. Allow the quiche to cool and firm slightly a few minutes before cutting.

Serves 8.

TEMPURA

Tempura is an unusual way to entertain with natural foods. It can be used as an appetizer or main course, served cooked at the table or made ahead and kept warm in the oven.

A fun way to cook the tempura at the table is to have the various vegetables ready and arranged on a platter on a small side table. Announce what the vegetable is and fry a batch of that particular item. Let the vegetables drain briefly and then pass them around the table. Guests are always amazed at how fresh vegetables taste, because the quick cooking seals in flavor.

TO MAKE TEMPURA

Mix together at least one hour before cooking time:

½ CUP WHOLE WHEAT FLOUR
½ CUP CORNMEAL
½ TEASPOON SALT
1 TABLESPOON SOY FLOUR
¾ CUP OR MORE WATER (You can use more or less, depending on how thick you like the batter.)

Refrigerate the batter.

At the end of the hour remove the batter from the refrigerator. If it is too thick, thin it with water.

Have ready a combination of the following vegetables cut into bite-sized slices or pieces.

ZUCCHINI OR SUMMER SQUASH   CAULIFLOWER
BROCCOLI   GREEN PEPPERS

RECIPES

YAMS	MUSHROOMS
GREEN ONIONS OR ONION RINGS	EGGPLANT
CARROTS	

Dry the vegetables before dipping into the batter. If the batter does not seem to stick well, first roll the vegetables in flour. After dipping in flour, drop into hot fat in a preheated deep fryer, being careful not to crowd the pieces. When the pieces are fairly well browned, remove and drain on paper towels.
This amount serves about two and can be increased as desired.

VARIATIONS
- Tempura only one type of vegetable such as mushrooms, and while they are still hot, sprinkle with grated cheese, either cheddar or jack. This makes a good appetizer.
- ½ teaspoon onion powder can be added to the tempura batter for a different and delicious taste.
- Fruit fritters can be made by using pieces of fresh fruit such as apples, peaches, pears, and bananas. A mixture of equal amounts of melted butter, honey, and a dash of cinnamon thrown in can then be drizzled over them for a yummy dessert.

USING SOY MEAT SUBSTITUTES

A number of tasty and useful meat substitutes made from soy are on the market today. These can be used to make a large number of main dishes. One of my favorites is by FEARN; it's called "Sesame Burger Mix." It's full of healthful ingredients, is very inexpensive, and makes tempting entrees. There are numerous similar products on the market; just be sure you are buying a healthful one. Some of them contain sugar, artificial colorings, and artificial preservatives and flavorings.

Most of these mixes come in a dry powdered form. You add water and sometimes an egg to reconstitute them, allow them to sit until the liquid is absorbed, and then they can be used in any number of ways. They will extend meat (directions for doing that are always given on the individual product), or fried until crumbly, they can be used as a meat substitute in any hamburger recipe. They won't taste quite the same but with some creative thinking old hamburger casserole recipes can be remade into some interesting new dishes.

134

SESAME MEXICALLI SKILLET

In a medium-sized bowl mix together:
1 CUP SESAME BURGER MIX
1 EGG
½ CUP WATER

Stir together well and allow to set 15 minutes until the liquid is absorbed.

In a large skillet add:
¼ CUP SAFFLOWER OIL

Saute in the oil until soft:
ONE ONION, CHOPPED

Add and saute until crumbly:
THE RECONSTITUTED SESAME BURGER MIX

Add:
1 CAN DRAINED CORN
ONE CAN CHOPPED AND PARTLY DRAINED TOMATOES
SALT AND PEPPER

Optional additions:
1 CAN HOT OR MILD CHILI PEPPERS OR GREEN PEPPERS, chopped
GRATED CHEDDAR CHEESE can also be sprinkled on top just before serving.
Heat through and serve.

EGG PUFF ROULADE

A roulade is an elegant main dish. It is like a jelly roll, only instead of cake, you have a light, cheese-and-egg flavored shell. The filling is a seasoned vegetable mixture. This takes time and hard work, but for special occasions it's worth it.

TO MAKE THE ROULADE SHELL:

Melt in a saucepan
¾ CUP BUTTER

RECIPES

Saute in melted butter:
½ ONION, CHOPPED FINELY

Saute until onions become clear.

Add ¾ CUP WHOLE WHEAT FLOUR.

Stir for several minutes until the flour cooks and then add:
1 ½ CUPS OF WARM MILK.

Stir until well blended. If you have a hard time getting it blended—if it turns lumpy or if you're just in a hurry—put the mixture into the blender and liquefy.

Add to above mixture:
4 EGG YOLKS
⅓ CUP GRATED PARMESAN OR ROMANO CHEESE

Blend mixture well and allow to cool slightly.

In another bowl beat until soft peaks form:
4 EGG WHITES.

Carefully fold egg whites into other mixture.

Grease well with liquid lecithin a 10'' X 14'' jelly-roll pan. (A jelly-roll pan is just a cookie sheet with sides.) Sprinkle the sheet lightly with 2 tablespoons fine bread crumbs. Spread egg mixture over the pan evenly. Bake in 400° oven for 20 minutes or until puffed and lightly browned.

While it is baking, prepare one of the suggested fillings. When roulade is baked, allow to cool for a few minutes. Carefully loosen edges with a knife and turn out onto a tea towel.

Spread hot filling over roulade and roll up jelly-roll fashion. Pour sauce over roulade and serve immediately. If it cannot be served immediately, reheat in a microwave or keep warm in an oven set on low.

You can also slice the roulade with a very sharp knife, nicely arrange the slices, and pour the sauce over them.

MUSHROOM AND SPINACH FILLING

Melt in a large skillet:
2 TABLESPOONS BUTTER

Saute in the butter
2 ½ CUPS CHOPPED MUSHROOMS

Add and steam until wilted:
1 POUND SPINACH THAT HAS BEEN CLEANED AND CHOPPED
After spinach is wilted, drain mixture of excess moisture and mix with ¼ cup of the sauce on p. 138.

SHRIMP OR CRAB VARIATION
Add to above mixture:
½ CUP OF EITHER FLAKED CRAB OR SMALL SHRIMP

ZUCCHINI AND EGGPLANT FILLING

Place in a large skillet

¼ CUP OLIVE OIL
1 SMALL EGGPLANT THAT HAS BEEN PEELED AND FINELY CHOPPED
2 SMALL ZUCCHINI, FINELY CHOPPED
½ TO ¼ CUP FINELY CHOPPED ONION

Saute until all vegetables are very tender.

Add:

2 CUPS CANNED TOMATOES THAT HAVE BEEN PUREED IN A BLENDER
2 TEASPOONS HONEY
1 TEASPOON LEMON JUICE
¼ CUP CREAM

Cook, stirring occasionally over low heat until sauce is very thick.

Spread over roulade, roll up, and top with the following sauce.

ROULADE CHEESE SAUCE

Melt in medium saucepan:
¼ CUP BUTTER

Stir and cook a few minutes:
¼ CUP WHOLE WHEAT FLOUR

Add and blend well:
2 CUPS WARM MILK

Cook, stirring constantly over medium heat until thick.

Add:
¼ CUP GRATED PARMESAN CHEESE
DASH SALT AND PEPPER
Stir until blended.

This sauce can be made up to one day ahead, stored in the refrigerator, and reheated when needed.

BROILED AND SKEWERED VEGETABLES

This looks so lovely to serve and is quite tasty though very easy to make. If you don't have skewers, you can make them by cutting a metal coat hanger apart and just using the bottom piece. Then take steel wool and scour off all the paint on it. These are also nice to make for picnics or barbecues in the summer.

Cut any of the following fresh vegetables into bite-sized pieces and place on a skewer.

ONIONS
MUSHROOMS
CHERRY TOMATOES
GREEN PEPPERS
ZUCCHINI OR OTHER SUMMER SQUASHES
EGGPLANT

Brush with olive oil and sprinkle on an herb salt such as SPIKE.

Broil for 5 to 10 minutes, turning once.

Place skewers on a mound of hot rice and serve.

VARIATION
On an oven-proof platter, place hot rice, push vegetables off skewer, sprinkle on top ½ to 1 cup of grated jack or cheddar cheese, and heat briefly in oven or microwave until cheese melts.

FETTUCINI ALA YVONNE

Though this recipe does not take much actual preparation time, you must plan ahead because some of the ingredients *must* be at room temperature when it is made, and this takes several hours.

Set out the following ingredients several hours before you are ready to use them and allow them to come to room temperature:

4 EGGS
½ CUP WHIPPING CREAM
1 CUP HALF-AND-HALF

Just before you are ready to serve the fettucini prepare the following ingredients and place each in a bowl near where the fettucini will be tossed:

1 ½ CUPS RAW, THINLY SLICED FRESH MUSHROOMS
¼ CUP MELTED BUTTER
½ CUP ROMANO CHEESE, GRATED
½ CUP PARMESAN CHEESE, GRATED
2 TABLESPOONS MINCED PARSLEY
DASH OF SALT AND PEPPER

The fettucini must be served very hot. If you are brave, you can have your guests seated at the table and toss it there. If you're a little shaky, do it in the kitchen and then bring it to the table. The important thing is to have everything ready before the noodles are cooked.

First heat an oven-proof serving dish in a 350° oven. I think the best item

RECIPES

for this is a 9'' X 13'' glass cake pan. Cook the pasta according to the recipe on the box. My favorite is sesame fettucini noodles but sesame spaghetti works well also. One pound will serve 4-6. While pasta is cooking, beat together cream and eggs and have all the ingredients ready. When pasta is done, quickly pour into a colander to drain, but do not rinse. Take hot serving platter from oven and turn pasta on to it. Toss pasta with butter. Then pour egg and cream mixture over and toss until well coated. The heat from the hot pasta will quickly cook the raw eggs. Add mushrooms, cheese, parsley, salt, and pepper. Toss quickly and serve immediately.

Notes on fettucini: To toss the pasta quickly and well, I would recommend the special wooden, long-pronged pasta forks. If these are not available, use very heavy, large-sized cooking forks or large salad forks. Do not attempt to do this with spoons or small utensils, because they cannot bear the weight of the pasta, nor will they allow you to do the tossing as quickly as is necessary.

Though fettucini purists would shudder at fettucini being reheated in a microwave if it chills or if some is leftover, the only difference will be a firmer sauce.

Fettucini is especially good served with a spinach salad.

18
Meats in
Moderation

RECIPES

WAYS TO CUT DOWN ON MEAT CONSUMPTION

If we wish to cut down on meat consumption but still not become a vegetarian, there are two ways we can do it. One is to eat lower on the food chain, which means to eat a protein source that does not take as much grain to produce as beef does. Fish is an excellent example of this type of food, and I'll be giving a number of recipes for it.

The other method is to do ethnic cooking. No one else in the world eats meat in the same way Americans do. A brief survey of any ethnic cookbook shows that most cultures make their meat usage go much further than we do. For example, the American way to cook chicken is to fry a couple of whole chickens for the family dinner. The oriental way would be to take a couple or one chicken breast and to stir-fry the bits of meat with a variety of vegetables and rice, and feed a whole family from a few pieces of meat.

Oriental cooking is a perfect illustration of a sensible way to use vegetables and meats to lower meat consumption.

In practice you can add meat or seafood in small pieces to stir-fried rice (p. 129) or to any of the basic pasta (p. 130), or soup dishes (pp. 107-112) to change them from a vegetarian to a meat-efficient dish.

Explore ethnic cookbooks to see other ways of doing this.

CHICKEN AND VEGETABLES VELVET

Marinate together for 30 minutes:

2 BONED CHICKEN BREASTS, CUT IN SMALL PIECES
1 TEASPOON CORNSTARCH OR ARROWROOT POWDER
2 EGG WHITES
1 TEASPOON GINGER, FINELY CHOPPED
2 TEASPOONS HONEY

In a large wok or frying pan, first stir-fry in a little oil:
4 CUPS OF CHOPPED VEGETABLES SUCH AS CARROTS, CELERY, ONIONS, OR ZUCCHINI.

When they are in season, fresh snow peas are absolutely delicious.

Stir-fry vegetables until barely tender and remove to another plate.

Add chicken breasts in marinade and stir-fry until chicken is cooked.

Add and stir in well:
¼ CUP WATER

Add:
Cooked vegetables.
Heat through and serve with cooked brown rice.

NOTES ON STIR-FRYING AND COOKING IN A WOK
By definition stir-frying usually means to cook quickly over a small intense heat source in a wok. Vegetables and meats cooked this way do not become overcooked, and they retain their crisp, yet tender texture.

A wok, a large cooking utensil with high curved sides, is usually used to stir-fry. It was developed in the orient to make maximum use of the small amount of fuel available for cooking.

It is not necessary to have a wok to do stir-frying; you can use a large skillet. However, a wok is a wonderful cooking utensil and one I highly recommend. It works well to cook so many things in—to stir-fry, deep fry, or steam in—and it looks nice to serve from at the table. Cooking with one is fun.

BASIC METHODS FOR COOKING FISH

Both methods work well with inexpensive white fish: perch, turbot, whiting, whitefish, etc.

PAN FRYING
Thaw fish and dip into flour; gently pan fry in a skillet in melted butter over medium heat until flesh turns solid and flakes easily.

TOPPING FOR PAN FRY: Even the most inexpensive fish pan fried and topped with this topping will taste elegant.

In a small skillet melt:
¼ CUP BUTTER

RECIPES

Add and saute until mushrooms are tender:
1 CUP CHOPPED MUSHROOMS
½ TEASPOON TARRAGON

POACHING
Make a basic poaching liquid from:

¼ CUP WATER
¼ CUP CHICKEN OR FISH STOCK
JUICE FROM ½ LEMON
½ TEASPOON EACH OF PARSLEY, ROSEMARY, BASIL, AND MARJORAM

Place in a baking dish and add pieces of thawed fish. Cover pan with foil and bake in a 350° oven for 15 minutes to half hour, or until fish is solid and flakes easily.

LOUIS SEAFOOD SALAD

I always used to think that you had to have lots of expensive crab and shrimp to prepare a Louis-style salad. An excellent one can also be made using any inexpensive white fish.

Poach and cool one pound of any inexpensive white fish:

PERCH
WHITEFISH
TURBOT

Flake the fish and remove any bones or skin.

Arrange the chilled fish and the following ingredients on a platter of cleaned and torn, bite-sized pieces of Bibb or leaf lettuce:

2 OR 3 HARD-COOKED EGGS THAT HAVE BEEN CHOPPED OR SLICED
1 DICED CUCUMBER
1 TOMATO, DICED OR SLICED
1 CAN ARTICHOKE HEARTS
1 CUP BROCCOLI PIECES THAT HAVE BEEN BOILED BRIEFLY AND CHILLED

Pour over salad the Louis dressing on the next page.

LOUIS DRESSING

Blend together:

¾ CUP PLAIN YOGURT
⅓ CUP MAYONNAISE
⅓ CUP CHILI SAUCE
DASH TABASCO, SALT, AND PEPPER

SAVANNAH SPLIT PEA AND SEAFOOD CHOWDER

I got the idea for this soup while visiting that wonderful city and eating in an old inn previously frequented by pirates. You can vary the spiciness by adjusting the amount of hot pepper you add.

Heat together:

2 CUPS SPLIT PEAS THAT HAVE BEEN COOKED UNTIL VERY SOFT (The measurement is for the *cooked* split peas not the dry ones that aren't cooked.)
1 28 OZ. CAN PUREED TOMATOES
1 SMALL CARTON HEAVY CREAM
¼ TEASPOON OR MORE CAYENNE PEPPER
½ CUP FLAKED CRAB MEAT
½ CUP SHRIMP

More seafood can be added if desired.

Heat gently throughout and serve.

WEST INDIES PERCH SUPPER

Thaw, pat dry, and place in baking dish:
1 POUND PERCH (Any other white fish such as turbot, cod, or whitefish could also be used.)

Saute together a few minutes:
¼ CUP BUTTER

RECIPES

½ CUP FINELY CHOPPED ONIONS
3 CLOVES GARLIC, VERY FINELY CHOPPED
When onions are soft, pour butter, onions, and garlic over fish.

Place on top of this mixture:
1 LARGE TOMATO, FINELY SLICED
2 BAY LEAVES

Pour over all:
¼ CUP CHICKEN OR FISH STOCK

Sprinkle on:
DASH SALT AND PEPPER

Cover baking dish with foil and bake 20 minutes at 350°. Uncover and bake for 10 more minutes.

RED CLAM SPAGHETTI SAUCE

Saute in a large skillet in ¼ CUP OLIVE OIL:
3 LARGE CLOVES OF GARLIC, FINELY CHOPPED.

Add :
2 CUPS OF CANNED ITALIAN TOMATOES THAT HAVE BEEN PUREED IN A BLENDER
DRAINED LIQUID FROM TWO 7 ½ OZ. CANS OF CLAMS

Cook slowly for about 45 minutes until the sauce is thick.

Add:
2 TABLESPOONS MINCED PARSLEY
1 TEASPOON MARJORAM
2 TEASPOONS BASIL

Simmer gently for 10 minutes.

Add:
THE DRAINED CLAMS
Heat through and serve over sesame spaghetti.

19
Desserts

CARROT CAKE

This is my version of this original, all-purpose natural foods dessert.

Cream together:
5 EGGS
¾ CUP SAFFLOWER OIL
¾ CUP LIQUEFIED HONEY

In a separate bowl combine:

2 ¾ CUPS WHOLE WHEAT PASTRY FLOUR
½ TEASPOON SALT
1 TABLESPOON BAKING SODA
1 TEASPOON NUTMEG
2 TEASPOONS CINNAMON
1 TEASPOON CORIANDER

Mix together liquid and flour mixture.

Add:
¾ CUP RAISINS
¾ CUP CHOPPED NUTS: WALNUTS, PECANS, OR ENGLISH WALNUTS
2 ½ CUPS GRATED CARROTS

Optional: Add one small can drained, crushed pineapple.

Bake in a greased 9'' X 13'' pan for 45 minutes at 325°. Cool and frost with cream cheese frosting (p. 148), flavored with vanilla. Garnish with pecans.

Note: After this cake is made and frosted it freezes beautifully. The flavor even seems to improve. Freeze either whole or cut up in individual portions.

CREAM CHEESE FROSTING

This is the healthy substitute for whenever you would use powdered-sugar frosting. It can be flavored in many ways and is good on carrot cake, coffee cakes, and cinnamon rolls.

Blend together:
12 OZ. CREAM CHEESE
1 ½ STICKS SOFTENED BUTTER
¼ TO ½ CUP OR MORE LIQUEFIED HONEY
DESIRED FLAVORING

FLAVORING VARIATIONS
- 1 teaspoon of any of the following flavorings can be used: vanilla, almond, lemon, orange, or strawberry.
- ½ cup carob powder can be added to make a carob frosting.
- Chopped nuts, coconut, citrus rind, or dried fruits can also be mixed in or used as a garnish.

FRESH FRUIT MOUSSE

If you're looking for a dessert that is light as a cloud, creamy, and just melts in your mouth, this is for you. It can be made with any kind of fruit, fresh or frozen, and is a perfect summertime dessert.

Puree:
2 CUPS OF ANY KIND OF FRUIT SUCH AS STRAWBERRIES, RASPBERRIES, PEACHES, APRICOTS, BANANAS, BLUEBERRIES, ETC.

Add and mix in well:
½ CUP LIQUEFIED AND WARMED HONEY
Set this mixture aside.

In a small bowl soak ONE TABLESPOON UNFLAVORED GELATIN in 2 TABLE-SPOONS OF COLD WATER for a few minutes, then dissolve it with ¼ CUP BOILING WATER. Be sure all the gelatin dissolves.
Add 2 TABLESPOONS LEMON JUICE.

Add the gelatin mixture to fruit puree and also add:
1 CUP HEAVY CREAM

Mix well.

RECIPES

Beat:
4 EGG WHITES INTO SOFT PEAKS.

Carefully, but *completely* fold egg whites into the fruit mixture. This will take time so be patient.

Carefully pour mixture into your nicest glass bowl. Allow to set. The mousse can also be frozen if you want a frozen dessert.

After the mousse has set, it can be garnished. Take either whole, perfect strawberries or whatever fruit was used and arrange them on top in any desired pattern. Make a glaze out of ¼ CUP HONEY that has been heated until it is quite runny, and carefully brush the fruit with it.

Allow to chill a few minutes to set the glaze and serve. The mousse can also be put into small individual serving cups to set. Whipped cream can be used to decorate the top of a fruit mousse.

FONDUE

Though the popularity of fondues seems to have waned somewhat from its high level a few years ago, it's still fun.

Fondues and similar ways of eating are good for you in more ways than just the nutrition of good ingredients. Eating your food piece by piece and having to pause between bites is a tremendous aid to digestion. Most people gobble their food, sitting at the table and shoveling it in as fast as they can. Inadequate chewing causes digestive problems; eating too fast makes one swallow air, causing gas problems and discomfort. There is a time lag between the time food enters the mouth and the stomach feels full. If one eats too quickly the stomach will be filled long past the point of comfort before the brain receives the signal to stop.

Eating a fondue is also good for the digestion in that it is a relaxing way to eat. It is so much more fun to invite people to dinner if the food has something unusual about it. If you happen to have people over that you barely know, being able to talk about the food is a perfect icebreaker.

This imaginative way of serving healthful foods is a good way to introduce your family to products they may be unfamilar with. Plain yogurt straight out of the carton is not exactly something kids come home demanding as an after-school snack. But the way it is used in this dessert makes it a yummy food. Once your family has had a good experience with a particular healthy food, they will be more likely to try it in ways that are not as familiar.

FRESH FRUIT FONDUE

Fill a fondue pot or decorative bowl with one of the following:
- 3 CUPS OR MORE OF ANY PLAIN YOGURT THAT HAS BEEN BEATEN OR FLUFFED LIGHTLY, preferably a thick heavy brand, one that still has the cream in it rather than a low-fat type.
- 3 CUPS OF PLAIN YOGURT BEATEN WITH ¼ CUP HONEY, 1 TEASPOON VANILLA, AND ½ TEASPOON CORIANDER.
- 3 CUPS PLAIN YOGURT AND ¼ CUP HONEY.

Around the pot place bowls of sliced fruits that have been cut into bite-sized pieces:

PINEAPPLE	PEARS
APPLES	ORANGES
BANANAS	STRAWBERRIES, MAY BE LEFT WHOLE
PEACHES	

Then set out little bowls of date sugar, shredded coconut, and finely chopped nuts such as almonds.

PROCEDURE
Each person spears a piece of fruit on their fondue or other fork, dips it into the yogurt mixture, and then into the toppings.

ICE CREAM

The enjoyment of ice cream certainly has become much simpler since the days of Nero, the Roman emperor who employed slaves to run to far-off mountains to bring him snow that was then mixed with honey and fruit to make the first sherbet.

Marco Polo, the famous explorer and adventurer, brought an ice cream recipe back from ancient China that used milk instead of snow.

Only the very wealthy could ever taste this delight because of the difficulty of the freezing process.

Today things are different. Every grocery store has entire cases filled with frozen goodies, and several fast food chains devote themselves entirely to dairy delights. Americans take advantage of this by eating approximately 700 million gallons of ice cream per year or about sixteen quarts per person.

Though no one would argue that the availability of such a delightful treat is a good thing, some modern advances in the production of ice cream are not good. In the old days, when ice cream was made from milk, eggs, and fresh fruit, it was a healthful supplement to the diet as well as a delicious treat. However, today's ice cream often contains little food value and a lot of harmful ingredients. For example:

- Diethyl glucol, a chemical used in antifreeze and paint removers, is used as an emulsifier instead of eggs.
- Piperonal, a chemical also used to kill lice, is used in place of vanilla.
- Butyraldehyde, one of the ingredients of rubber cement, is used to make nut-flavored ice cream.

The list goes on and on, with perhaps the ultimate request being made by the industry recently when it asked the federal government to allow them to make ice cream with no dairy products at all. The request was denied, but the fact that it was made is amazing.

You don't have to eat a chemical mixture when you want ice cream. There are a number of healthful ice creams in natural food stores that are made with real eggs, cream, and honey. They all taste delicious. They may cost more, but you will be paying for the real thing and not a chemist's concoction.

Homemade ice cream is best of all. An electric ice cream freezer is one of the best investments you can make to assure yourself of a delicious dessert.

HOMEMADE ICE CREAM

For this recipe you will need a one-gallon ice cream freezer. For a half-gallon one, just cut the recipe in half.

Basic mixture:

Blend together in a large bowl:

4 CUPS WHIPPING CREAM
3 CUPS MILK
2 EGGS
½ TEASPOON SALT
1 CUP HONEY (Note on the honey: before adding the honey to the other mixture, warm it slightly until it is very runny, then it will blend with the other ingredients. Be sure it blends in well or it will glob up when you freeze and won't be mixed in.)

Add any of the flavor variations below and mix well. After flavorings have been added, pour mixture into ice cream freezer and add additional milk until the liquid comes to the fill line. Freeze according to the directions with your particular freezer.

FLAVOR VARIATIONS
- 1 package frozen strawberries
- 1 to 1 ½ cups of mashed fresh fruit: could be peaches, pears, strawberries, blueberries, etc.
- 1 cup mashed bananas, ⅓ cup chopped walnuts
- Any plain flavoring can be added, just one or two teaspoons such as vanilla, lemon, or almond.
- 1 tablespoon almond flavoring, ½ cup chopped almonds

YOGURT FREEZER CHEESECAKE AND VARIETY DESSERT

This is one of the most versatile dessert recipes I have ever created. The crust is delicious as is or used in place of a graham cracker crust in any recipe.

The dessert can be flavored in innumerable ways and used as a pie filling, or it can be layered with fruit as a parfait or served in bowls topped with fruit.

Let your imagination run wild.

153

RECIPES

CRUST

Mix together:
1 ¼ CUPS OAT FLAKES
⅓ CUP WHOLE WHEAT FLOUR
¼ CUP COCONUT (can be omitted)

Heat in small pan over low heat:
½ CUP BUTTER
2 TABLESPOONS HONEY
1 ½ TEASPOONS VANILLA

Heat through until butter melts and honey is dissolved. Pour liquid mixture over flake mixture and combine well. Butter a 10-inch pie plate or a 9" X 9" square baking pan. Press crust into it in a thin layer. Bake at 325° about 20 minutes or until lightly browned.

Cool piecrust and add the following filling.

BASIC FILLING

Beat together with electric beater until smooth and then pour into piecrust and freeze until firm:

1 CUP SOFTENED CREAM CHEESE
⅔ CUP PLAIN YOGURT
¼ CUP MILK POWDER
⅓ CUP LIQUEFIED HONEY (More can be added for a sweeter filling.)

FLAVOR VARIATIONS
- Any kind of flavoring can be added using about 1 ½ teaspoons per recipe, some to try include vanilla, lemon, and almond.
- One-half to one cup frozen fruit can be added such as strawberries, peaches, blueberries.
- Fresh fruit such as peaches or bananas, from ½ to 1 cup, can also be added.
- Fruit can either be added in pieces, or it can be pureed and then added to the basic mixture and blended in well.
- The filling can be made without fruit and flavored with either vanilla or almond, and then after it is chilled, cut into pieces and the

154

following fruit topping spooned over.

FRUIT TOPPING

Combine:
3 CUPS CHOPPED FRUIT SUCH AS STRAWBERRIES, PEACHES, BLUEBERRIES, FRESH
OR FROZEN
1 CUP OR MORE CHOPPED BANANAS
⅓ TO ⅔ CUP LIQUEFIED HONEY
¼ CUP DATE SUGAR

Note: Filling doesn't have to be frozen though it is easier to serve that way. When chilled, it becomes puddinglike and you can use it in a parfait or as a fruit-topped pudding.

EASY HEALTHY PIECRUST

Piecrusts have come a long way from Roman times when they were expected to act as a portable dish to keep meat sauces off one's fingers and clothes in the days of eating without silverware.

Nowadays we expect some lighter-than-cloud miracle. That is hard enough to achieve using white flour and lard, but it is absolutely impossible with whole wheat flour and vegetable oil.

However, piecrusts made with whole wheat flour can still be delicious. They can be very tasty and crisp, but they will not be flaky. The flaky texture comes from the fat melting between the layers of flour in the presence of high heat. Unsaturated, unrefined oils cannot form those layers so don't frustrate yourself trying to make one.

Whole wheat crusts should be handled quickly and as little as possible because the gluten content in the flour will cause the crust to become tough. (The same motions you use to knead bread to make it strong will also toughen the gluten in piecrusts.)

After trying many healthy piecrust recipes, I have found the following one easiest and most delicious.

Note: This is for a one-crust pie: a two-crust pie made with whole wheat flour is far too heavy. If you want some kind of topping on the pie use the crumb pie topping (p. 159).

RECIPES

Mix together:
1 ½ CUPS WHOLE WHEAT FLOUR
½ TEASPOON SALT
Option: ½ cup of the flour can be replaced by any of the following nuts that have been finely ground:

WALNUTS   SUNFLOWER SEEDS
PECANS   WHEAT GERM
ALMONDS   SESAME SEEDS
FILBERTS

This option is especially delicious when used for fruit pies. For example, walnuts are yummy in a crust for apple pies, and almonds are fantastic with the pear pie. Extra wheat germ, sesame, or sunflower seeds are nice with mince or pumpkin pies.

Slowly drip over the flour mixture:
⅓ CUP SAFFLOWER OIL

Cut the oil in with a pastry blender until well mixed. Add stirring as little as possible until a dough is formed:
4 OR MORE TABLESPOONS WATER

Whole wheat piecrusts, or any crusts for that matter, are difficult to roll out. You really don't need to. It's much easier to butter a pan and press the dough in. Press this crust in a buttered pie pan thinly and uniformly, avoiding overthick areas.

The crust can then be used for any of the following pies or for the quiche (p. 132). If you need a precooked crust, bake in a 350° oven for 20 minutes or until lightly browned.

OPTIONS
- You can also use unbleached white flour for the recipe or half unbleached white and half whole wheat.
- If you can find a product called Sterling Flour Blend, a mixture of soy, wheat, and carob flours, it makes good piecrusts.
- A nice combination of ingredients in a piecrust consists of using equal amounts of whole wheat flour, unbleached white flour, and **ground walnuts.**

156

APPLE PIE

What I love most about apples is their smell. My grandmother's farmhouse in Nebraska always smelled like apples. When you came in the back door, the warm, spicy fragrance reached out, enveloping you in welcome.

A more ancient or more widely used fruit can hardly be found. From accusations as the forbidden fruit in the Garden of Eden to present study by archeologists, apples are thought to be the most ancient fruit eaten by man. They are mentioned in the Bible, the *Hindu Code of Manu,* the *Egyptian Book of the Dead,* and Hesiod's *Theogony.* They are found at the sites of ancient excavations and are pictured in some of the oldest stone carvings.

It is no accident that apples have enjoyed this long and useful history. High in vitamins and minerals, including the controversial anticancer vitamin B_{17} in their seeds, apples are a good source of fiber and an excellent aid as a teeth cleansing snack. They deserve a prominent place in the diet.

As a substitute for gooey, sugar-laden junk desserts apple pie rates as a winner. Easy to make and enjoyed by everyone, it's an appropriate dessert with almost any meal.

APPLE RAISIN PIE

Slice, leaving the peels on for added nutrition and fiber content:
7 CUPS APPLES FOR AN 8-INCH PIE
8 CUPS FOR A 9-INCH PIE

In a medium-sized kettle, place vegetable steamer with water below, put apples in and steam until apples are tender but not soft and mushy. Remove apples from heat; place in large mixing bowl.

In another bowl combine well:
½ CUP HALF-AND-HALF
3 TABLESPOONS HONEY (You can add more or less honey depending on how sweet you like your pie and how tart the apples are.)
1 TABLESPOON ARROWROOT FLOUR OR CORNSTARCH
¼ CUP RAISINS

RECIPES

1 TEASPOON CORIANDER
1 TEASPOON CINNAMON

Pour liquid mixture over apples and mix well. Pour into an uncooked whole wheat piecrust. Bake at 350° for 35 minutes. An additional bit of cinnamon and a few raisins can be sprinkled on top for garnish when the pie is done.

VARIATIONS
- Raisins can be left out.
- Other additions that can be used instead of raisins:
  ¼ CUP CHOPPED NUTS SUCH AS WALNUTS OR PECANS
  ¼ CUP FROZEN OR FRESH BLUEBERRIES
- Half the apples can be replaced by pears or peaches.
- 2 to 4 tablespoons of date sugar can also be added to the pie.
- Don't forget how delicious apple pie is topped with homemade vanilla ice cream.

PEAR PIE

A few miscellaneous notes about pears might be helpful. They are one of the few fruits that are best picked green and then ripened in a cool, dark place (never a refrigerator) at around 70°. When they are ripe, their color changes from green to yellow, and they develop a definite pear smell.

If pears are to be cooked as in this pie recipe, they should be used while still firm though ripe. If pears are allowed to get too soft, one good use for them is to peel and cut out the badly browned sections and to puree the remainder in the blender. The end product then can be sweetened with honey to taste, chilled, and eaten as a pear sauce, a product similar to applesauce. The plain sauce can be used to substitute up to half the amount of bananas called for in banana nut bread recipes or any recipe calling for mashed bananas.

PIE PROCEDURE

Slice into a bowl:
5 CUPS PEARS, firm, not overripe, peeled and cut into slices.

158

In a saucepan combine the following mixture:

⅔ CUP NATURAL, UNFILTERED APPLE JUICE
1 TABLESPOON ARROWROOT FLOUR OR CORNSTARCH
2 TABLESPOONS HONEY
1 TEASPOON CINNAMON
½ TEASPOON NUTMEG
1 TEASPOON CORIANDER
2 OR MORE TABLESPOONS DATE SUGAR (optional)

Cook, stirring occasionally over medium heat until slightly thick.

Add sliced pears and cook a minute more.

Pour into prepared, unbaked piecrust.

The pie can be either baked as is or topped with Crumb Pie Topping (p. 159).

VARIATIONS
Peaches can also be made into a pie using this recipe.

CRUMB PIE TOPPING

When making a pie with a whole wheat piecrust, a double crust is hard to work with and too heavy. If you want a topping, however, the following one is quite nice to sprinkle over a fruit pie. It works especially well with apple and pear pies.

Blend the following ingredients with a pastry blender until crumbly:

2 TABLESPOONS WHOLE WHEAT FLOUR
2 TABLESPOONS BUTTER
5 TABLESPOONS DATE SUGAR
½ TEASPOON CINNAMON
½ TEASPOON CORIANDER

Sprinkle over the top of the pie and bake.

RECIPES

FRUIT COBBLER

Every recipe box needs at least one quick and easy dessert for that unexpected dinner guest. This is a healthy one.

Place in an 8'' X 8'' baking dish:
2 16 OZ. CANS OF FRUIT OR 1 QUART OR MORE OF HOME-CANNED FRUIT
or
4 CUPS CHOPPED FRESH FRUIT
(My favorites in this are home canned with honey peaches or cherries.)

Mix together in a saucepan:
⅔ CUP OF JUICE EITHER DRAINED FROM THE FRUIT OR APPLE JUICE
1 TABLESPOON OF ARROWROOT FLOUR OR CORNSTARCH
2 OR MORE TABLESPOONS HONEY DEPENDING UPON THE SWEETNESS OF THE FRUIT USED.

Cook liquid mixture until thickened and pour over fruit.

Make a double batch of Crumb Pie Topping (p. 159) and sprinkle over fruit.

Bake in 350° oven 20-30 minutes or until heated through and topping begins to brown.

Serves 6
● Nice served hot with vanilla ice cream, half-and-half, or real whipped cream.

RAISIN PECAN PIE

When the children of Israel came to crown David king in Hebron in biblical times, part of the food they brought with them for the huge feast was raisins. These delicious little nuggets of sun-dried grapes have been cultivated in that part of the world since 6,000 B.C. with the Egyptians being the first raisin makers.

Not only were raisins a delicacy in times of feasting, but ancient

160

literature often mentions their use for strengthening battle weary soldiers and to revive almost dead and exhausted messengers in their travels across the desert. When modern day backpackers stop to revive their energy by munching a handful of raisins, few probably realize how ancient an art that is.

Raisins supply this quick, natural energy because they are 64 percent fructose, a natural fruit sugar. They also contain amounts of dietary fiber, iron, calcium, phosphorus, and potassium.

Raisins are also a prime ingredient in many healthful breads and desserts. Below is my husband's very favorite pie. It's the one recipe he said I had to learn before we got married. My version is a healthy adaptation of a Texas family favorite shared with me by a wonderful cook, my mother-in-law.

PIE PROCEDURE
First make a healthy pie shell; bake and cool.

RAISIN PECAN PIE FILLING

Cream together in a large heavy saucepan:
¾ CUP HONEY
3 EGG YOLKS
Add:
1 CUP RAISINS
1 TABLESPOON BUTTER, CUT IN BITS
2 TEASPOONS ARROWROOT FLOUR OR CORNSTARCH
Cook over medium heat until the mixture begins to thicken.

Turn off the heat and add:
1 CUP CHOPPED PECANS
1 TEASPOON VANILLA

Turn heat back on to medium and cook a few more minutes. Pour thickened filling into prepared pie shell.

Make a meringue by beating the remaining egg whites. When almost firm drizzle 1 or 2 teaspoons of liquefied, warmed honey over the meringue and continue beating to blend in. Top the pie with meringue and bake at 425° for five minutes until the meringue is golden. Allow the pie to cool 15 minutes before serving. Start out serving small pieces because the pie is very rich.

20
Snacks

NOTES ON SNACKING

We may not get up in time for breakfast; dinner and lunch may come at times when we're involved in important projects, but everybody has time for snacking.

Snacking has a bad reputation because of the sugary, empty foods associated with it, but it can be good for you if you're snacking on healthful items. For some people, such as hypoglycemics, snacking is a necessity to keep the blood-sugar level high.

Be careful when purchasing some of the new "natural" snack items that you aren't just paying an inflated price for something in a new package. The new interest in natural foods has produced some tasty snacks that are available in bulk. You might try some of these:

NUTS: Try the unsalted, unroasted kind. Almonds are the lowest in calories and fat and high in protein, making them a very good snack. Others to try include cashews, walnuts, and filberts.
Nuts roasted in tamari (soy sauce) are also delicious.
Don't forget good old peanuts, either raw or in the shell.

SEEDS: Sunflower or pumpkin seeds either in the shell or out are a healthful snack that's high in minerals.

GRAINS: Corn, wheat, and other grains are now being deep fried, salted, and sold as a snack food. Some are very delicious. They are sold under names such as "trigos," which are wheat, "cornuls," which are corn. Many people are already familiar with roasted soybeans.

DRIED FRUIT AND RAISINS: These are delicious as a snack, but be careful not to eat too much because of high calorie and sugar content. Also brush teeth after eating dried fruits because they cling tightly to teeth and can cause decay.

GORP MIXTURES: These are the mixtures of nuts, seeds, and toasted grains. You can either buy the mixtures already made up or you can buy a combination of ingredients you enjoy and make your own mixture.

DON'T FORGET THESE: Fruit, cheese, cold vegetables, and granola.

163

CARAMEL CORN WITH VARIATIONS

Not a junk food, nutritious, and at only 75 calories per cup, popcorn classifies as an excellent snack. It's also one of the more historical snacks; the American Indians munched on it long before the first European set foot on this continent.

Popcorn is a completely different variety of corn than the regular table corn because of its unique ability to pop when heated. This mechanism is not fully understood, but it is believed that steam develops in the kernel. When sufficient pressure is reached, the kernel explodes and expands to thirty times its original size.

The following recipe is great for kid's parties and for use as a Halloween treat.

In a saucepan with high sides combine:

¾ CUP HONEY
¼ CUP SORGHUM (If you don't have sorghum, you can use all honey.)
1 TEASPOON VANILLA

Cook over high heat, stirring constantly until the mixture registers the soft ball stage on the candy thermometer, if you like your caramel corn chewy, or the hard ball stage, if you like it crisper. If you don't have a thermometer, just cook it about 5-7 minutes.

Immediately pour boiling honey over:
3 QUARTS OF POPPED CORN
Toss quickly to coat the corn.

While the mixture is still warm, but has cooled about 10 minutes, it can be pressed into a greased mold to make a popcorn cake or formed into popcorn balls.

VARIATIONS
You can add numerous additional ingredients to the popped corn before tossing it with the honey, for example:
- 1 CUP RAISINS, ½ CUP MIXED NUTS, ½ CUP SUNFLOWER SEEDS
- ½ CUP CHOPPED PECANS, 1 CUP CAROB CHIPS
- 1 CUP LARGE COCONUT FLAKES, ½ CUP FINELY CHOPPED DRIED PINEAPPLE

NATURAL NACHOS

This is a great snack and especially fun as an appetizer before a casual dinner party. Make them up in a big 9" X 13" cake pan and serve in the middle of a coffee table. Give all the guests a fork to dig in and watch how quickly the whole thing disappears.

In a large 9" X 13" glass cake pan pile:
2 LARGE PACKAGES OF NATURAL CORN CHIPS, TAMARI CHIPS, CORN PUFFS, OR WHATEVER YOU LIKE

Sprinkle over the top:
1 TO 2 CUPS GRATED CHEESE (MAKE IT ANY NATURAL CHEESE, MOZZARELLA, JACK, CHEDDAR, OR A COMBINATION OF THESE.)

Options for on top:
1 SMALL CAN CHILI PEPPERS, either mild or spicy, depending upon your preference. Seed the peppers and chop them well.
¼ CUP CHOPPED FRESH MUSHROOMS

Heat in a 350° oven until the cheese melts and serve immediately. If desired, red chili sauce can also be served alongside or sprinkled on top.

FRUIT LEATHERS

These are great as a snack for children or backpacking, and unlike what you would imagine from the commercial variety, very inexpensive to make. This is also a good way to use up leftover bits and pieces of canned fruits, and it's a good way to use up imperfect scraps of fruit left over from canning.

Puree in a blender:
2 ½ CUPS OF FRUIT
1 OR MORE TABLESPOONS HONEY, TO DESIRED SWEETNESS
If needed, ¼ cup or so of water can be added to get the fruit to begin to blend.

165

RECIPES

Pour pureed mixture over a lightly greased cookie sheet and spread evenly. Place in oven at its lowest temperature for 4 to 7 hours. The time varies depending on the oven temperature and the amount of moisture in the fruit. Keep checking the leather and when the moisture is gone and the leather feels dry on top, take it out, roll up, and cut into strips. It can be stored in tightly sealed glass jars.

VARIATIONS

- You can combine several kinds of fruits such as apples and strawberries, bananas and strawberries, peaches and pears.

- Raisins and dates can be added to any fruit leather.

- Spices such as coriander, cinnamon, and nutmeg give the leather a nice flavor.

- A favorite combination of mine is 2 ½ cups apples, 3 pitted dates, 2 tablespoons raisins, ¼ teaspoon cinnamon, and ¼ teaspoon coriander.

NATURAL CANDIES

Endless combinations of natural candies can be made by combining any assortment of healthy ingredients with something to make them stick together. Try whatever sounds good to you, or copy the ingredient list from some ready-made candies, proportions aren't very important in most of them. Here are two varieties to get you started.

CREAM CHEESE DELIGHTS

Cream together in a medium-sized bowl:
1 SMALL 4 OZ. PACKAGE OF CREAM CHEESE
1 TABLESPOON RAW SESAME SEEDS
2 TABLESPOONS FLAKED COCONUT
1 TABLESPOON HONEY
2 TABLESPOONS DATE SUGAR, CHOPPED DATES, OR RAISINS
½ TEASPOON LEMON EXTRACT

166

2 TABLESPOONS FINELY CHOPPED CASHEWS

Form into little balls, roll in flaked coconut, and chill.
Makes 12 balls.

GARBAGE GOODIES

In a base of:
½ CUP NATURAL PEANUT BUTTER ADD:
2 TABLESPOONS HONEY

Add ½-cup total of any of the following items in any combination you choose:

GRANOLA	DATE PIECES
COCONUT	DATE SUGAR
WHEAT GERM	NUTRITIONAL YEAST
SUNFLOWER OR SESAME SEEDS	MILK POWDER
RAISINS	TOASTED SOY NUTS

Form into little balls and chill.
They can also be rolled in carob, coconut, or date sugar.
Makes about 10 pieces.

Note: Both taste even better if made about a day ahead and allowed to mellow in the refrigerator.

21
Spice It Up

HERBS, SPICES, SEASONINGS, AND SAUCES

Seldom do we realize the king's ransom and treasures we have in our spice cabinets. Lands were discovered, nations built and crumbled, countless fortunes made, and lives lost—all over spices.

Not only do spices do marvelous things to food, but the study of their history, uses, and folklore can be a fun and fascinating hobby.

In natural cooking especially, spices, seasonings, and sauces can make a huge difference between something that is blah or unforgettable. This section will give you a potpourri of hints and instructions to put your food in the unforgettable or at least edible category.

NOTES ON HERBS AND SPICES

Be brave, experiment, and try herbs and spices you've never tried before. Try one at a time and use enough of it so you can see what it tastes like. Crush the spice in your hands before adding it to the food, smell and taste it. Become familiar with it and think what else it would taste good in. Disregard all cookbook instructions about being subtle and using only a little bit of a spice, especially the ones that say you shouldn't use so much of a spice that you are able to taste it. If you can't taste it, why use it? I love the flavor of tarragon in gazpacho and basil in spaghetti sauce. What would dill cream be like, if you couldn't taste the dill?

An understanding of the makeup of most herbs and spices helps in understanding how to store and use them. If the spice is a leaf, as many are, it's very delicate, somewhat like a tea. If you boil a tea for several hours, what happens? The delicate flavor leaves and all that is left is a bitter aftertaste. The same thing happens if you boil spices for a long period of time; they lose their delicate taste and become bitter. You should always add spices the last ten minutes or less of cooking, and never let the liquid boil while they are in it.

It's a little different if the spice is in a hard coating like an allspice, cloves, or peppercorns. These must be boiled to extract their flavor. Or you can crush them in a mortar and pestle before adding to the food.

Since heat releases the flavors of spices, they should be stored, preferably in a dark, cool place. Storing them above or very close to the stove will cause most of their flavor to dissipate before they are used. The flavor in spices also is not long lasting. If you have some spices longer than a year or two, they will have either lost considerable flavor or have none left at all.

169

If a natural foods store near you sells spices in bulk, buy them in small quantities. I have found their spices to be very good tasting and usually inexpensive.

If you have the room, grow an herb garden. Nothing is more delicious than fresh herbs. At the end of the summer, you can dry your own herbs to enjoy all year long. Home-dried herbs are far superior to commercial ones, because the large spice companies dry their herbs with heat, thus saving time but losing flavor.

Instead of buying combinations of spices, make up your own from herbs bought in bulk. A favorite of mine for any kind of baking is 2 parts cinnamon, 1 part each ground nutmeg and coriander, and ½ part ground anise.

If you feel you must buy a seasoning salt, don't buy a chemical concoction but a natural one that is made from herbs such as SPIKE, which can be bought at the natural foods store.

SAUCES IN COOKING ESPECIALLY AS A SUBSTITUTE FOR CANNED SOUP

I used to think that I couldn't cook without canned soup. Every other recipe I used seemed to call for either tomato soup, cream of celery, or cream of mushroom soup. Either canned soup or those little foil packets you added water to were the only way to make sauce, I thought. When I became interested in natural foods and realized what chemically worthless products I'd been using, I panicked. I had no idea what to substitute. I had always heard that sauce making was hard.

I laugh to think how wrong I was. After a little experimenting, I found sauces not only easy, but inexpensive and tasty. The following is my basic recipe whenever the need for any sauce arises.

BASIC SAUCE WITH VARIATIONS

In a fairly heavy skillet melt:
3 TABLESPOONS BUTTER.

Add and cook for several minutes:
3 TABLESPOONS FLOUR.
This step of cooking the flour is very important, because the flour has to

170

have time to cook and lose its raw taste. Many homemade sauces have a pasty taste because this step is omitted.

After several minutes add:
2 ½ CUPS HEATED MILK.

Stir it in with a whisk or wooden spatula. Try to get it stirred in smoothly, but if that doesn't work, don't worry about it and think you can never make sauces. Sometimes lumps just happen. If they do, pour the lumpy mess into the blender a few seconds, and you will have a smooth, velvety sauce.
Season with salt and pepper and you have the most basic white sauce; the variations from here are endless.

Some basic seasonings:
Bay leaf
Thyme
½ an onion that has been sauteed in butter until soft.

To make the sauce a little fancier any of the following can then be added, either alone or in combination with the others:
1 CUP SAUTEED MUSHROOMS (This is the substitute for cream of mushroom sauce.)
¼ CUP GRATED CHEESE (Best to use Parmesan or Romano. They will dissolve the best.)
1 CUP CELERY, SAUTEED UNTIL VERY SOFT (Substitute for cream of celery soup)

Another combination to add to the basic sauce consists of: 2 bay leaves, 1 teaspoon garlic powder, ½ sauteed onion, 3 tablespoons tomato puree, pinch of basil, and pinch of marjoram.

Epilogue

A few evenings ago some friends and I were in our local ice cream parlor. I was not sipping herb tea; I was devouring a hot fudge sundae. One of my cooking class students walked by, and she was honestly shocked. If she hadn't hurried away, I would have liked to have explained a bit to her.

In college, a Coke, candy bar, and potato chips were my standard meal. Tonight was the first time I'd eaten a sweet in months, and I was sharing this one. For me that's progress. My family does eat much more nutritiously; I'm not anemic anymore or twenty pounds overweight. I do feel my eating habits reflect my Christian commitments, but my appetite hasn't been perfected yet.

I still love coffee. I hate nutritional yeast, and soybeans give me gas. I remind myself that in the area of foods, as in all of life, we're still pilgrims and a pilgrim hasn't arrived at his destination. He's just moving towards it.

I was raised a Presbyterian and I like benedictions. Here is my benediction and prayer for everyone attempting to make whatever they eat or drink or whatever they do work together to the glory of God. "May God himself, the God of peace, sanctify you through and through. May your whole spirit, soul, and body be kept blameless at the coming of our Lord Jesus Christ. The one who calls you is faithful and he will do it" (1 Thess. 5:23, 24).

Appendixes

Bibliography, References, and Resources

There is so much more—so many books, references, and resources. This will give you a few ideas that have been helpful to me.

If you cannot find the books listed, write to the following bookstore. If the book is not out of print, they will be able to send you a copy immediately if they have it in stock or order it for you. Please ask them for postage and price information.

Special Order Department
Chinook Book Shop
210 N. Tejon
Colorado Springs, CO 80903

GENERAL BACKGROUND BOOKS

Airola, Paavo, Ph.B., N.D. *Are You Confused?* Phoenix: Health Plus Publishers, 1971.

Cheraskin, E., M.D., D.M.D., and Ringdorf, W.M., Jr., L.M.D., M.S. with Arline Brecher. *Psychodietetics.* New York: Bantam Books, 1974.

Hunter, Beatrice Trum. *The Natural Foods Primer.* New York: Simon and Schuster, 1972.

Kirschmann, John D. *Nutrition Almanac.* New York: McGraw-Hill, 1975.

Rohrer, Virginia and Norman. *How to Eat Right and Feel Great.* Chicago: Tyndale House, 1977.

BOOKS RELATING TO HUNGER

Mooneyham, Stan. *What Do You Say to a Hungry World?* Waco, Tex.: Word Books, Inc., 1975.

Sider, Ron. *Rich Christians in an Age of Hunger.* Chicago: Inter-Varsity Press, 1977.

Simon, Arthur. *Bread for the World.* Paramus, N.J., and Grand

Rapids, Mich.: Paulist Press and Wm. B. Eerdmans, 1975.

BOOKS ON THEORY AND PRACTICE

Ewald, Ellen Buchman. *Recipes for a Small Planet.* New York: Ballantine Books, 1973.
Lappé, Frances Moore. *Diet for a Small Planet.* New York: Ballantine Books, 1971.

BOOKS ABOUT CHILDREN

Davis, Adell. *Let's Have Healthy Children.* New York: Harcourt Brace, 1972.
Feingold, Ben F., M.D. *Why Your Child Is Hyperactive.* New York: Random House, 1974.
Lansky, Vicki. *Feed Me, I'm Yours.* New York: Bantam Books, 1977.
Lansky, Vicki. *The Taming of the C.A.N.D.Y. Monster.* Wayzata, Minn.: Meadowbrook Press, 1978.

BOOKS ABOUT NATURAL EATING AND HEALTH

Airola, Paavo, N.D. *How to Keep Slim, Healthy, and Young with Juice Fasting.* Phoenix: Health Plus Publishers, 1971.
Dufty, William. *Sugar Blues.* New York: Warner Books, 1975.
Jacobson, Michael F. *Eater's Digest: the Consumer's Factbook of Food Additives.* New York: Doubleday, 1972.
Winter, Ruth. *A Consumer's Dictionary of Food Additives.* New York: Crown Publishers, 1978.

NATURAL FOOD COOKBOOKS

Ford, Marjorie Winn; Hillyard, Susan; Kooch, Mary Faulk. *The Deaf Smith Country Cookbook.* New York: Collier Books,

1973.

Gorman, Marion, and deAlba, Felipe P. *The Dione Lucas Book of Natural French Cooking.* New York: E.P. Dutton, 1976.

Hooker, Alan. *Vegetarian Gourmet Cookery.* San Francisco: 101 Productions, 1976.

Jordan, Julie. *Wings of Life.* Trumansburg, N.Y.: The Crossing Press, 1976.

Longacre, Doris Janzen. *More with Less Cookbook.* Scottsdale, Pa.: Herald Press, 1976.

Robertson, Laurel; Flinders, Carol; and Godfrey, Bronwen. *Laurel's Kitchen.* New York: Bantam Books, 1976.

Sunset Cookbook of Breads. Menlo Park, Calif.: Lane Publishing Co., 1977.

Sunset Seafood Cookbook. Menlo Park, Calif.: Lane Publishing Co., 1977.

RESOURCE GUIDE

COOKING AND KITCHEN ITEMS

Write and ask to be placed on their mailing list. You will receive excellent catalogs.

Williams-Sonoma
Mail Order Department
P.O. Box 3792
San Francisco, CA 94119

Kitchen Bazaar
Mail Order Division
4455 Connecticut Ave., N.W.
Washington, DC 20008

Garden Way Catalog
1300 Ethan Allen Ave.
Winooski, VT 05404

FOR SOME NATURAL FOODS

First a store that carries a complete line:

Old Towne Organic Grocery
2607 W. Colorado Ave.
Colorado Springs, CO 80904

FOR SOME MISCELLANEOUS ITEMS THAT ARE HARD TO FIND
(such as natural bouillon and natural flavorings)

Barths of Long Island
Valley Stream, NY 11582

FOR THE BEST DATE SUGAR

Shields Date Gardens
80-225 Highway 111
Indio, CA 92201

FOR THE CROCK STICK, THE EASY WAY TO SHARPEN KNIVES:

Knife Gallery
462 Templeton Gap
Suite 151
Colorado Springs, CO 80907

For all the above places, write for current price and postage
information.

Index

INDEX

FROM GOD'S NATURAL STOREHOUSE

FROM GOD'S NATURAL STOREHOUSE

FROM GOD'S NATURAL STOREHOUSE